I AM CANADA

BEHIND ENEMY LINES

World War II

by Carol Matas

Scholastic Canada Ltd.

Toronto New York London Auckland Sydney
Mexico City New Delhi Hong Kong Buenos Aires

A Dear Canada Book. Published by Scholastic Canada Ltd.
SCHOLASTIC and I AM CANADA and logos are trademarks
and/or registered trademarks of Scholastic Inc.

Library and Archives Canada Cataloguing in Publication

Matas, Carol, 1949-
Behind enemy lines : World War II / Carol Matas.

(I am Canada)
ISBN 978-0-545-99066-0

1. Canada. Royal Canadian Air Force--Gunners--Juvenile fiction.
2. World War, 1939-1945--Prisoners and prisons, German--Juvenile fiction.
3. Prisoners of war--Canada--Juvenile fiction. 4. Prisoners of war--Germany--
Juvenile fiction. I. Title. II. Series: I am Canada

PS8576.A7994B44 2012   jC813'.54   C2011-905479-5

6 5 4 3 2 1   Printed in Canada 114   12 13 14 15 16

The display type was set in Happy Daze.
The text was set in Minion.

First printing January 2012

To the 168 Allied airmen shot down and sent to Buchenwald, and to all the other airmen to whom we owe our freedom.
And also to my family who, along with myself, might not even exist had Hitler prevailed.

Chapter One
June 3, 1944

From my rear turret I got a glimpse of our attacker, a twin-engine Ju88, coming in for the kill.

"Corkscrew port! Go!" I shouted over the intercom to the skipper.

There was flak everywhere — little black cloud bursts all around.

Skipper relayed back, "Down port!"

We dove. I'd say 1,000 feet easy.

I started to fire and kept firing as we corkscrewed.

"Changing," Skipper said. He pulled out of the dive.

Then "Up port," came over my intercom as he climbed as steeply as he could manage with the lumbering Lanc.

I was almost out of ammo when suddenly the Ju broke away. I swung around, straining to see.

"Rolling." Lew was converting the climb to starboard. "Up starboard."

Before Lew could call "Changing" I felt the hit. A starboard engine flared. I couldn't see a thing. I

1

was ready with my Browning but now had to wait for Stan to feather the engine. Sure enough he did and the fire went out. That's when I saw the two fighters, but too late. We took another hit. There was an explosion so loud my ears started to ring.

For a moment I held my breath, not knowing how bad it was, just that the entire plane had shaken as if we were one of those souvenir snow globes and someone had picked us up and dropped us. But then that unseen hand picked us up again and started to shake us and shake us.

The skipper said, "Starboard wing's all lighted up, fellows. Bail out, bail out." His voice was calm, as if he were telling us to have a cup of tea.

I decided to get out the rear door — turning my turret would take too much time — plus this way the others could follow me out. But the door wouldn't come loose, it was jammed. *"For fanden, fandens ogsaa!"* I muttered in Danish.

That's when Max appeared with an axe and broke the lock — he must have been there and come back with the axe, but I'd been trying too hard to open the door to even notice him.

I snapped my parachute pack onto my harness and then Max pushed me out, the bright white lights bursting through the darkness all around me.

The wind jerked me away from the plane with

such force that for a moment I couldn't even think what I had to do next. Then I heard my training sergeant's voice. "Dreamboy. Hey, Dreamboy. Don't forget to pull your cord when you jump. Dreamboy. Hear me?" Yup. I heard him. I reached for the rip cord. Panic washed over me. It wasn't there. It wasn't there! I was going to smash into the earth. Any second now. Did I even have time to deploy it? And then I heard another voice, my sister's. "Sam. Can't you tell right from left? Honestly! Lucky thing they aren't training you as a navigator!"

I reached for the rip cord on the other side. And there it was! I pulled.

The parachute deployed. It tugged me back up before I started to float slowly down. I tried to get my bearings. I was high enough up still — that was good.

The night was bright. A cloudless sky. The moon almost full.

My chute began to sway in a circular motion. I couldn't control it. Then I looked down and saw what looked like water. I knew that if I landed there I'd probably drown, pulled down by the weight of the harness and the canopy. The day they'd trained us in parachute control I'd been playing cards in the back of the room with Max, because who wanted to think about the fact that maybe we'd need to bail out. We preferred to ignore what Max liked to call "negative thoughts." Facts, more like it, but too late now.

As I got closer to the water I realized it wasn't water but a large field of wheat. The noise of the aircraft faded. So did the bursts of anti-aircraft fire. The quiet of the night surrounded me. Time seemed to slow. It almost seemed peaceful. And then with a pretty hard bump, I was on the ground. I rolled and then managed to right myself. I seemed to be in one piece.

I hit the release button on my chute and wriggled out of it. One thing I had paid attention to — the orders about what to do if you survive a crash. I knew I only had minutes.

I had an escape kit with maps and a compass and a passport photo tucked into one of the large front pockets of my battledress jacket, but I had no time to use any of that now. First thing was to hide the parachute so the enemy wouldn't know there was an airman alive somewhere around here. But there was nowhere to hide it. I pulled off my leather gauntlets and heated gloves and finally the silk gloves, so I could reach into my pants pocket. I grabbed my knife and began to cut up the chute so I could hide it better. It seemed to take forever and the silk was harder to slice than I would have thought, but it didn't help that my hands were shaking. I gave up when I had it in a few pieces. I dug a shallow pit with my hands and then stomped on the chute to flatten it down. I knew I had to get out of there fast. The Germans on the ground would have seen *H Hall* go down in flames and they'd be out after us even before our kite's position was radioed in by the Ju88 pilot.

I was starting to sweat. And that's when I realized I needed to get out of some of the gear I'd put on before the flight, just to keep from freezing to death in the minus-30 temps we'd get in the turret. I started by getting out of my lined leather flight suit, then stripped off layer after layer, which seemed to take forever, until I was down to my battledress jacket, my trousers, plus my thick cable-knit sweater that I tied around my waist. I had to dig a shallow pocket in the earth all over again and stuff the rest of my gear in as best I could.

It was still quiet. Too quiet. Where were my crew? Had any made it? There was a huge ball of flame not far off, which had to be our downed kite — it was bright enough that I could easily see where I was. Hunkering low, I decided to run away from that light. The farther away from the evidence the better. I dashed through the wheat field and suddenly got this overwhelming feeling of strangeness. The air smelled sweet. The stars were shining. And the fact that a war was raging all around seemed almost impossible.

When I reached the edge of the field I saw a copse of trees just ahead. I lunged into it. And it was only a few seconds later that the quiet was pierced by the sound of cars travelling along a road somewhere close by. I had no doubt who they were looking for. I decided the best thing to do was to keep moving. That's when I heard the groan. The night was so quiet I couldn't have missed it. I inched cautiously over toward the sound — after all, it could as easily be a German as one of us. But when I peered around a tree, there was Bill, our navigator. He was trying to get up but couldn't.

"Need a hand?" I whispered.

He broke into a grin when he saw me. That was Bill. It would take more than getting shot down and — maybe a broken leg? — to dampen his spirits.

"I propose we get out of here," he said.

Bill had been in law school before signing up; sometimes he still talked like a lawyer.

"Let me look at that," I said.

I'd spent a lot of time going on call with Pops

over the years, watching him treat people. And picked up a thing or two. I examined Bill's leg as gently as I could.

"Sprained ankle," I said.

"Lucky for me that it's the football player who found me, then."

"Lucky for you," I agreed, as I put my arm under his and shouldered his weight. Still, he couldn't help but put his foot down as we walked — it must have been excruciating, but he never uttered a peep of protest or cried out or anything.

I could hear Coach's words in my head as I half-carried Bill. "Someday you'll thank me for this, Fred." Coach could never bother to say *Frederiksen.* I always wondered why he didn't just call me Sam. Surely that was short and sweet. But no, it was always, "Pick it up, Fred!" Or, "Are you pretending to push a pram, Fred?" as we ran round and round the track at the start of football season and then did more push-ups than seemed reasonable.

Bill and I staggered on until just before dawn and by then I *was* thanking Coach. We saw some farmhouses but didn't stop at any of them, since we wanted to get as far away as possible from the crash site. Finally we reached another copse of trees and I decided we needed to stop. I was exhausted. I helped Bill settle on the ground and I sat beside him, each of us resting against a tree.

"We need to get you to a doctor," I said.

But he was out cold.

Chapter Two
June 4, 1944

I woke with a start. I must have finally dozed off for an hour or so because now it was obviously morning.

Standing over me was a boy of maybe thirteen or fourteen. He had his hands on his hips and was glaring at me. *"Réveille-toi, idiot!"* he hissed. I'd actually been very good at French in high school. I knew right away that he was saying, "Wake up, idiot!"

"Have some respect for your elders," I snapped back in English. All right, maybe eighteen wasn't that much older than he was, but after all I'd been through the night before, I was feeling pretty rough. I guess I should have been worried or maybe even scared that I'd been found, but for some reason I wasn't. I'm not sure the boy understood what I said, but I'm pretty sure he understood the tone.

"Shhhh," he cautioned. "There are Germans everywhere." Or something close to that at any rate. Tenses were always my downfall, so he could have said "are" or "were" — I couldn't be sure.

I replied in French. "Where are we?"

And he obviously didn't mind my accent because he answered right away. Something about Perry?

He pointed at Bill and said, "He needs a doctor."

I looked over. Bill was out cold and his colour was terrible. I scrambled over to him and saw to my horror that he'd been bleeding. His jacket was thick with blood. Gingerly I peeled back a corner of the jacket and saw that he'd taken a hit from shrapnel on his right side just over his ribs. He must have already lost a lot of blood.

"Wait here," said the boy and then ran off.

Well, I couldn't move Bill now, but could I trust this kid?

I looked around. The spot we'd found wasn't as protected as I'd thought. We were sitting in a copse of about half a dozen trees and were quite near a road — a small one, but a road neverthe-less. As I peered out from behind the tree I could see a village not far away and a small farmhouse just to the south. In fact we were surrounded by people. People who could spot us and turn us in. I'd heard stories from downed airmen of amazing heroics from ordinary Frenchmen and women who had risked their lives to help these fellows get back to England. On the other hand, we had all heard about the collaborators. Established escape routes out of France were compromised time and again by someone who wanted a dozen eggs in exchange for the life of an Allied airman. I scrambled away from the trees toward a high wall. From there perhaps I could see the boy before he saw me and decide whether he was going to turn us in or help us.

Quickly I surveyed my surroundings. The wall I was leaning against was an old village wall. I pulled myself up and peeked over. Just beyond the wall was a road and a main street. Shopkeepers were starting to open up. I ducked back down as fast as I could. I realized that I was far too exposed where I was, so I made a run back into the trees.

I needed to scout the rest of the land around us. As a gunner, my training was mostly honing my skills as a lookout — in fact, I realized suddenly, last night had been the first time I'd actually shot my guns in combat. My job for the most part was to spot the enemy and tell the skipper and hope he could lose the fighters before I had to shoot. We all knew that a slow Lancaster bomber was no match for a fast German fighter — and my Browning was no match for their guns.

I could see a rather large farmhouse and barn to the west. I wondered if that was where the boy had come from. But what had he been doing out so early? Had he been looking for survivors of the crash? I thought we'd put a good distance between ourselves and the downed plane, but maybe not far enough.

He's either gone to get help, I thought, or to get some advantage with the Germans by turning us in.

I watched the large farmhouse for a few minutes but saw no activity. The small farmhouse was equally quiet. I took stock. I was very thirsty. I was hungry. Well, that was normal at least. And Bill was out cold. I needed to make a decision. I thought back to the boy and the look on his face when he spoke to me. He seemed genuinely concerned for our well-being — and perhaps too young to put on such a convincing act? I decided to risk it.

I sat down against the tree. I'd better be ready for a long day, I thought. And a run, carrying Bill possibly, if need be. I suddenly remembered my first-aid kit and pulled it out of my trouser pocket. There was a dressing I could use on Bill, but I was lucky I had more knowledge about medicine than most because of Pops being a doctor. I realized that if I pulled the material from Bill's jacket away from the wound, it would start the bleeding all over again. A doctor would be able to clean the wound out properly and then bandage it, so I decided to leave it alone.

I took out my escape pack and had a look through it, placing the items on the ground in front of me. There was a map of France; some French money, which might come in quite useful so I slipped it into my back pocket; a small compass and a plastic water bottle which I also put aside for later; tablets for purifying water; a tiny razor and shaving soap; malted-milk tablets — two of which I ate right then, although I could hardly swallow them I was so thirsty. And of course some pictures of me in civvies so I could use them in a fake passport. I used the razor to cut the insignia off my battledress jacket but would need a regular shirt as soon as I could beg, borrow or steal one.

Out of the corner of my eye I noticed something. I looked up and saw activity from the large farmhouse to the west. A young woman came out and walked over to the barn. Just as that was happening I heard a roar from the road and looked over there. I couldn't see them, but there must have been trucks and cars parked there because I didn't hear the sound of just one car. And the only people who had gas for that many cars and trucks were Germans. Had I stumbled onto some kind of headquarters?

I shoved everything into my pack and put it back in my jacket. And then I saw a German soldier walk out of the front door of the farmhouse. My heart caught in my throat, my breath came in short gasps. It was one thing to see the enemy from a kite. It was quite another to see them up close and real. For a minute I almost thought I'd throw up.

It seemed that for now we were trapped where we were. If we moved we'd be spotted for sure. I hoped the boy wasn't from that farmhouse.

That hope didn't last long. The boy walked out just after the soldier did, and then sauntered away toward the road leading to the village. Had he already given us away?

Bill moaned and stirred. I had to have a plan. I took out the map and tried to figure out where in France we could be.

As I studied the map I suddenly remembered where we'd been just before we'd crashed. We'd been flying a typical zigzag route home, hard on us because our instinct was to head straight for the Channel and away from the enemy. Just before the shooting started we were about to turn east toward the coastline and the Channel. I stared at the map. It was full of small villages. I scanned for anything that looked like Perry and then stopped when I noticed a small village called La Perrière, just north of Le Mans. If I could get Bill patched up, maybe we could make our way south until we got to Spain, the way they explained it to us in our briefings, and then back to England. I knew there was an invasion coming soon. I wanted to be part of it. And so did Bill.

But who was I kidding? Bill was in no shape to go anywhere and if we couldn't get him to a doctor so the wound could get cleaned, it could become infected and Bill could die.

The sound of trucks and cars moving along the road made it clear to me that we were well and truly trapped, with the road on one side of us and the open fields on the other. There was nothing to do but wait. And hope.

Chapter Three
June 4, 1944

It suddenly occurred to me that Mom would be getting a telegram saying I was missing in action. And if I couldn't get word to anyone soon, after a certain amount of time had passed there would be another telegram saying I was presumed dead. I thought about our house on Scotia Street, and how the telegram would be delivered. It might be a hot day, so maybe Mom would be on the front porch shelling peas, or in the kitchen baking, or maybe not even at home because she was working for the Red Cross every day packing care packages for POWs. And Pops probably wouldn't be there. He'd be at his office or out on a call — he was extra busy now that so many doctors were in the fight. Mom always said thank goodness for his ulcer! And what would poor Jenny say when she got home from school?

One big adventure. That's what I'd thought when Air Marshal William Bishop came to our school and talked to us about joining the RCAF as flyers.

By the time he was finished I couldn't wait! I guess I never really thought I'd end up like this. Shouldn't I have known? Shouldn't I have had a premonition or something? Instead, just yesterday, everything had seemed normal. Max had been teasing me, as usual. "Talking to yourself, Sam? Praying?"

I'd looked up from my camp bed, embarrassed. I'd been muttering aloud. *What do we do today, Sam?* *Change the world, Pops.*

"Nah," I answered quickly. "Just hummin' a tune."

I wasn't going to tell Max that it *was* a kind of habit, the way we started the day at our house, my dad asking me the same question every morning at breakfast, and me giving the same answer — the one he'd taught me to give — change the world, make it a better place.

I started to sing "Boogie Woogie Bugle Boy" at the top of my lungs just to prove to Max that I'd been singing, not talking to myself.

"Hey, cut that out!" Phil yelled.

So I toned it down as I threw on my gear and grabbed my kit.

Come to think of it though, I *was* nervous. And so was most of the crew, because our flight time had been changed at the last minute. I knew I wasn't the only one to worry when that happened. Did it mean good luck or bad? Were we now doomed to be shot down or was the change the thing that was going to save us? And since this was only our fifth sortie into enemy territory, maybe there was no such thing yet as "usual." We knew the invasion was coming soon, but not yet. It was June 4, 1944, and we were part of the vanguard preparing for that invasion, hitting rail yards and roads and making sure the enemy couldn't get to the Front when the invasion came. Out target was the railway yards in Trappes. Our way home was a pretty complicated route and not straight back by any means, which made me even more nervous.

I stood on the tarmac and looked up at *H Hall* and felt my stomach turn over. I suddenly thought about Jenny, and how she clung to me the last time I left home and how she cried. And how she gave me the little Pooh Bear that I always kept in my pocket for luck. Winnie for Winnipeg.

I reached into my pocket to give the bear a squeeze, the way I always did before an op. It wasn't there! And no time to go back for it. My heart sank. Actually I guess I should have known right then and there that trouble was coming for me, for us.

When it was time to go, Lew turned to us and, as he'd done just before every flight, said, "Tallyho, lads!"

We replied in unison, "Tallyho, Skipper!"

I winked at Max. We loved the way the British flyers talked, so calm and collected, and the way they acted and reacted too. I had all the confidence in the world in Lew and was happy to put my life in his hands.

Everything last night had seemed as routine as it could be, though, considering we were flying over enemy territory, being shot at and then dropping 16,000 pounds worth of bombs! I mean, after our drop we had no hits by flak, although as usual it was pretty darn scary flying though a blizzard of ack-ack. Still, no fighters on our tail, although there were plenty of them around us. At around 0200 hours it was quiet, and I was beginning to think that we were going to be lucky with our fifth op.

Lucky?

As dad would say, *"Ikke rigtig"* — not really.

"Penny for your thoughts."

I almost jumped out of my skin. Bill was awake.

"I was just thinking about how we ended up here — I had a kind of bad feeling . . . " I replied.

"Me too," he said, his voice quite weak. "But then I do every trip." He groaned. "Where are we?"

Count on the navigator wanting to know exactly where we were, no matter how weak he was.

"A small village called La Perrière," I answered.

I hated to worry him, but figured he'd better be prepared. "A kid found us — he said he's gone for help, but I saw a German soldier come out of the same farmhouse he did. We might be in for it."

Bill looked down at his ribs and then over to me.

"Am I hit bad?"

I nodded. "You need a doctor."

"I guess I could turn myself in — worst case, a prisoner-of-war camp and some medical help." He thought for a moment. I didn't say anything. Only he could make this decision.

"What did you make of the kid?"

"Seemed okay."

"I think I'll take my chances," Bill said.

Chapter Four
June 4, 1944

It was only minutes later that the boy turned up again.

I searched for the words. How did I ask him if he'd turned us in? I said, "Your sister is friends with the Boche?"

He actually spat. "Francine. She is," he replied. And then he used some words I didn't recognize and I'm pretty sure they weren't complimentary.

Of course this could have been an act to get us to trust him. I looked at him more closely. He was tall and thin with dark curly hair and big brown eyes. He had an air about him — like he noticed things, like he was sharp.

"You need to stay here until night," he told us, noting that Bill was awake. "Then I'll take you to that farmhouse" — he pointed to the small one south of us — "and get him a doctor."

He noticed my map. "Ah, excellent!" he said. And then he tapped where we were — just as I thought — the village of La Perrière. He moved his finger to a spot on the map just to the north of the village. "A farmhouse just south of this crossroads," he said. "The Resistance will meet you there."

"No," I shot back. "I'm staying with my friend."

He shook his head. "One man to hide is enough in that place."

He put a small basket down beside us and uncovered it. There was a carafe of wine, a couple of hunks of bread and a large piece of cheese. "Wait until dark," he said.

He looked around, got up and then sauntered away toward the town.

"Think it's poisoned?" I said to Bill.

"It would be if this were a Bogart movie," he replied. I was glad he still had his sense of humour. "Anyway, I'm not hungry — you go crazy."

"What about the kid?" I asked. "Do we trust him?"

"He could have handed us in by now," Bill said. "Unless he wants us to lead him to other downed airmen. But with me injured there's not much chance of that, so all in all I'd say, yeah, probably."

I wished the kid had brought us some water. I was so thirsty that after I forced Bill to take a few sips of wine I drank the whole carafe in a few gulps. Then I devoured most of the food after making sure Bill got some small bits down him.

It was hot, and with that and the wine, I guess I must have dozed off a few times, and so did Bill before night finally fell. In between I planned my route so that once it was night I'd know where I was going after I got Bill to the farmhouse.

Finally it was dark enough to move. I helped Bill up and put his arm round my shoulder. This time he was even weaker than last night, and heavier. We staggered through the field until I found a rough path that led to the farmhouse. We got there and knocked. The door flew open and an elderly man and his wife welcomed us in. She spoke mostly in French, but I was able to make out the gist of it.

"Please, please," she said. "You are our guests now. Up the stairs a room is ready." She was very short and thin and her white hair so wispy it stood almost straight up. Her husband was small too. The woman led the way.

It wasn't easy getting Bill up those stairs and he couldn't help but let out a few small groans as he put too much weight on his ankle. I eased him onto the bed. Right away a young man I assumed was a doctor slipped into the room. "Let's have a look," he said.

He shooed us all out and I went downstairs to share a glass of beer with the older man. His wife brought me some bread and sausage. It was pretty greasy but I was way too hungry to care.

They watched me eat with pleasure and then the doctor called down for help. I wanted to go but the wife wouldn't let me. "A woman's job," she said. Her husband and I sat silently together until she returned.

"The doctor has cleaned the wound out," she said. "We'll take care of him. You go now."

I wasn't leaving without saying goodbye so I went up the stairs two at a time and entered the room. Bill was shirtless, his ribs bandaged, his ankle bandaged, looking pretty pale.

"It appears I have landed a cushy assignment here," he said to me.

"Looks like it," I said.

"I'll be drinking wine and telling war stories in no time," he added. "My only wish would be a glass of cold water."

I grinned. "Looks like you'll have to make do with beer." I paused. "Take it easy."

"You too."

I left the room, thanked my hosts, and slipped out into the dark.

I'd never felt so alone as I did at that moment, standing there in the night without Bill. But I had no choice. So far the kid had been as good as his word. Now I had to find the Resistance.

I made my way north, giving a wide berth to

the nearby farmhouse and the German's car parked outside. I kept off the roads and travelled across the fields. It was slow going and different than my panicked run of the night before, but I'd made it through the crash without injuries so I sure didn't want to break a leg now. I heard the planes overhead about an hour into my walk, the crack of anti-aircraft fire and the sounds of cars and trucks on the road nearby. I wondered how the fight was going and when the Allied invasion would start. I took note that it was now June 4 and reminded myself to keep track of the date.

It was another beautiful night, warm and clear, without any chill in the air at all. I must have been walking for a few hours when I spotted a farmhouse just south of a crossroads, as the boy had described. Of course, I couldn't be positive it was *the* farmhouse, but it was in about the right place. There were no lights on. The house was surrounded by a ring of trees and I stood behind one of them so I could observe any movement.

"*Arrêtez-vous!*" said a voice behind me, low and quiet. I spun around. The moon and the stars gave enough light for me to see that a man was pointing a gun at my chest. I threw up my hands, just like in the movies, and said, "Don't shoot!"

Chapter Five
June 4, 1944

"Come with me," the fellow said, changing from French to perfect English — English with a very upper-class British accent.

I really had little choice. He motioned me toward the barn beside the house. I hoped against hope that he was part of the Resistance, or another downed flyer, and that I was about to find help. Or be able to offer help.

We moved quietly to the barn and as we got there the door opened and another man let us in. I could see that there was a small light on, a hand-held lamp near the centre of the barn, and that's where we headed. The man with the gun asked me my name and my rank. He was as tall as me, over six feet but thinner, and had a hat pulled well over his eyes. He spoke softly so that his voice wouldn't carry. I had been instructed that I could freely give out the information he'd requested, but nothing else unless I was certain I was with friends.

"Sergeant Sam Frederiksen," I said. I also spoke quietly.

And then the other fellow spoke. He looked to be older than me but not old — maybe twenty-five or so? He had red hair and blue eyes and freckles and a round pleasant face. But his expression was grim when he looked at me. He was stocky and quite a bit shorter than me, but something about him made it clear he was not to be trifled with. He had a distinct American accent, and asked me such a crazy question that for a minute I thought he must be joking.

"Who's the best player on the Yankees?"

"What?" I said.

"You heard me."

"I don't know," I answered honestly.

"A plant," he said to the British fellow with the gun. "Shoot him."

I heard the gun being cocked. "Wait a minute, wait a minute," I gasped, heart pounding. "Just because I don't follow baseball doesn't mean I'm a plant! I'm Canadian! Ask me anything about hockey — anything!"

The Yank looked thoughtful for a moment. "Who's the best player on the Boston Bruins?"

"Bill Cowley," I answered without a moment's hesitation.

The Yank scowled at me.

My heart sank. Was this it? Would I be killed by my own people?

"And the Montreal Canadiens won the Stanley Cup over the Chicago Black Hawks, four to zero," I said.

"Anyone knows that," said the Yank.

"Maurice Richard, nicknamed The Rocket, scored five goals in the first round, and in game two of the finals, a hat trick," I said. And for good luck I added something that I doubted any double agent would know. "And the Winnipeg RCAF Bombers lost the Grey Cup to the Hamilton Flying Wildcats, twenty-three to fourteen, last fall."

The Yank nodded. "Okay," he said, "but as for who's the top player on the Bruins — it's obviously Herb Cain, not Cowley."

"That," I replied with some dignity, "is a matter of opinion."

The Yank winked at the other fellow and put out his hand to me. "Ben Webber," he said.

"Flight Lieutenant John Thompson," said the Brit as he put his gun away. "The others won't be telling you their names. Best that way. And no titles between us, just first names." And as he said that, out of the gloom appeared six or seven more men.

"He's all right," John said to them in French.

The meeting didn't last long. And it took place in French spoken far too quickly for me to catch all of it. When the men left I was introduced to the fellow whose barn we were in, Raymonde.

John pointed to a bale of hay, indicating that was where I'd be sleeping. I lay down, but although I was tired I was far too revved up to sleep.

And there was one more thing keeping me awake. I was hungry. Really hungry. Pops used to tease me that one day he was going to submit me to medical researchers. He said no normal kid could eat the volume of food that I did and stay so fit. He thought if we could bottle my metabolism, we'd all make a fortune. In fact one of the best things about my gunner training was that I was able to take it in Manitoba, so I was often able to take my leave at home, and even to bring my pals along with me. Mom loved it when I brought friends home and she was able to cook up great big Danish dinners of *frikadeller* and parsley sauce and potatoes, and for dessert, cream cakes, which she'd manage by saving up all the cream from the milk and never letting Pops drink it in his coffee. Sometimes she would even make a *wienerbroed*.

Thinking about food made me think about Max. Danes and Jews had one thing in common for sure — food! Max used to go on and on about Montreal smoked meat sandwiches and bagels and kosher dills and something called brisket, which he swore would outmatch *frikadeller* any day. "Fried meatballs?" he'd scoff. "Try a hunk of meat cooked slow all day in sauce. Or if you want meatballs, try our sweet and sour."

Thinking about Max, I hoped against hope he hadn't been caught. Or killed. But for him caught might be worse. He'd told me some pretty gruesome stories about the Germans and how there were rumours that they were taking Jewish people to some kind of camps and killing them, but I told him over and over that no officer would ever condone such a thing. They're soldiers like we are, after all. And we soldiers have a code of honour that is never broken.

I must have finally drifted off or that blasted rooster couldn't have scared the heck out of me as dawn broke. Being a city boy, I had no idea just how loud the darn things were when they crowed in the morning, but I found out. I leaped up, staring around me wildly, until I realized where I was and what that awful noise was. Then I sank back into the hay.

We were brought breakfast soon after by a girl who looked to be around my age. She had her hair under a scarf and her cheeks were pale in the morning light, but she looked so pretty, and she smiled at me, and well, that picked me up.

I gobbled up the eggs and fresh bread and jam and boy oh boy did it taste good. It was gone in no time, though, and there were no seconds on offer. And my stomach was still rumbling.

John brought out a radio and placed it in front of Ben. "This was dropped by our chaps about a week ago along with some guns and explosives," he explained to me. "We're lucky Ben's been able to contact home and get some instructions. We're just waiting for our marching orders."

"Have you heard about any of my crew?" I asked.

"The plane went up in flames when it hit the ground," said John, "and by the time we got people there everyone was gone — except for two bodies — chaps that didn't make it out."

I nodded. I knew who one of them would be — Lew, who would have stayed with the kite to give the rest of us a fighting chance.

I suddenly realized I didn't even know if Lew had a sweetheart or brothers and sisters. Our talk had always been about the ops, the plane, the crew. I hoped that whoever else had escaped wasn't already in some French prison.

While I'd been lost in thought, Ben had been using the radio. He got up, hid it back in the hay and then said, "We have our work cut out for us. Starting tonight."

Chapter Six
June 5, 1944

It was then that the young boy who had first found me made an appearance. John spoke to him quickly, and he nodded and left. "A very good courier," John commented.

He and Ben got down to some serious planning for the night to come. I listened and tried to learn something.

After a very small lunch of some bread and cheese, and finally some water, which I was thankful for, I was put to work — making explosives!

I worked separating the material that the boy had brought with him into 5-inch pieces that looked like sausages as much as anything, but made me a lot more nervous than a sausage would have. I didn't know when one would blow up and take my hand off . . . or my arm. Ben noticed how carefully I was handling the stuff and assured me I didn't have to worry. To prove his point he picked up a handful of it and threw it against the barn door. I almost had a heart attack!

But nothing happened. He explained that it was a chemical reaction that would set it off. Tonight when we used it we would pinch the aluminum cover over it and that would begin the reaction.

As soon as the sun went down we headed out. It was warm and I figured that was why I was sweating, but in reality I was feeling pretty shaky. Yes, I'd had nerves before a flight, but this was different. I had no idea at all what to expect and no training to fall back on.

We had to pick our way forward because of the blackout, moving through the countryside without any light. As we continued we gained more members. I carried the explosives in a bag over my right arm. It seemed there was to be no apprenticeship. I was still in the fight, more Army now than Air Force, that was all.

We travelled for about an hour in the pale light of the moon, until we began to see more farmhouses and even some small villages. I could hear the sound of guns and then the sound of the planes, too, and anti-aircraft fire. I could even see some explosions off in the distance. More kites downed, no doubt. And then I saw the trains ahead and could hear one just leaving the yard. John was obviously in command, along with Raymonde, who was directing his men to certain areas. John pointed right at me and Ben and motioned for us to move ahead and place the explosives. I suppose the other men were covering us.

We got to the tracks. Trains loomed around us in the dark like monsters from my dreams when I was little. We could hear their engines chugging in the distance. I emptied the bag of explosives, still scared that the stuff would blow up right under us.

John and Ben, now joined by Raymonde, quickly placed the small devices along the tracks. It seemed to take them forever, and I kept thinking, just drop it and run! Finally they motioned for me to follow them and we headed away from the tracks. I could hear a train getting closer and closer and I wondered if some poor Frenchmen were going to die tonight because of my work.

We were running down a small gravel road when the first explosion went off. I could hear brakes grinding and then the sounds of metal crashing into metal and then some screams of pain and the angry sound of men shouting. I glanced back anxiously as we sprinted away, expecting to be surrounded any moment by Germans, but the sounds faded and no others took their place. Slowly the French fighters melted away into the countryside, and finally we arrived safely back at the same farmhouse we had started from. We hustled into the barn.

Ben contacted headquarters and reported in. Then I was ordered to get some rest. That was a welcome order and easy to follow. I fell into a deep sleep.

I dreamed my sister Jenny was crying because her best friend Liz had said something mean to her. I tried to console Jenny, telling her that she should tell Liz straight not to talk that way, and that they should make up, but Jenny cried harder and harder and then suddenly I woke up and realized that there really was someone crying nearby. The barn was still in darkness. I got up and followed the sound, which I finally realized was coming from the hayloft. Slowly I climbed the small ladder and then immediately stumbled over someone's legs.

"Ouch!" she protested.

"Sorry, sorry," I said. By then I had fallen over and was sitting beside her and could see it was the girl my age, from the farmhouse, the same one who had brought us breakfast yesterday morning.

"I heard you crying," I said. Or tried to say in French.

"My fiancé," she replied, sobs catching in her throat. "He's been arrested. Michel just ran over from the village to tell us. My fiancé and nine others." She paused. And with a definite edge to her voice she added, "Did you think no one would suffer for your little outing last night?"

"I'm . . . I'm sorry," I said to her.

"Sorry!" She gave a kind if snort, as if my apology was no use to her at all.

"Now wait a minute," I replied. "I ended up here because the Boche shot down my plane and there were six other men in it and two of them are dead for sure and maybe more. Do you want us to leave the Boche alone? You want us to leave them here so that they can pick up your fiancé or you or your family and do whatever they like to you at any time? Don't you want to be free?" I'm sure my French wasn't very good, but she seemed to understand me just fine.

"But he's innocent!" she cried.

"You're all in this war," I said. "There's the enemy and there's the rest and no one is just a bystander." I paused. "Well, I guess there are some who like the Germans, like the way they run things. Is your fiancé like that?"

"No!" she answered.

"Well then, he'll see it as being at war, won't he? Like being a soldier."

"Perhaps," she said.

It was getting light in the barn. The rooster crowed then and I could hear the others getting up.

"I'd best go fetch your breakfast," she said. She brushed away her tears and hurried off.

As soon as she had climbed down the ladder I followed her.

Ben saw me and gave me a wink, but I had something other than romance on my mind.

"We need to think about getting out of here," I said to Ben and John.

"Oh?" said John.

"The girl." I tilted my head toward where she'd gone.

"Marie-Claire," John said.

"I guess. Her fiancé has been taken hostage by the Germans. She's mad as all get-out. I'm pretty sure she blames us, and — "

"And if she gives *us* up," said Ben, finishing my thought, "in return maybe they'll let *him* go."

"That *is* one of the main reasons they take hostages," John confirmed. "It often works. I agree with young Sam here. It's time we moved along."

John told me to leave my battledress jacket behind and gave me a shirt he had scrounged from somewhere. He passed me some twine to tie my escape pack around my waist. After the girl had brought us our breakfast — which I made sure to wolf down — and she was back in her house, we simply walked off, Ben with the radio packed in a burlap sack.

But where could we go now?

Chapter Seven
June 6, 1944

We were only down the road a few hundred yards when Raymonde rode up to us on his bicycle and told us to follow him. After a ten-minute walk he turned down a rutted country lane — a good thing because the roads were starting to get busy. We could see a horse and wagon coming toward us and soon I had no doubt we would be seeing Germans too. All over the roads were the long metallic strips we called window that we dropped from our planes to confuse the enemy's radar. It was everywhere! You couldn't walk a foot without stepping on it. I wondered how the people even farmed without it getting tangled up in everything.

After half an hour we found ourselves at another farmhouse, this one with a large greenhouse. Raymonde motioned us to go inside. It was full of flowers — orchids and roses and even some cactus plants. We sat on the floor and waited. A tiny green lizard scampered down one of the wooden slats and along an irrigation pipe.

Soon Raymonde came in with an older man, maybe my *farfar*'s age, with a shock of white hair and bright blue eyes. He said, "Welcome. It will be my honour to be your host." I felt like I was at some fancy dinner party or something and could just picture him in a tuxedo looking like Cary Grant would if he were a grandfather.

Raymonde said, "I'll be sending the boy over with instructions for tonight's raid."

"Will he be safe?" I asked. "Your daughter knows all the men by sight, and most by name."

With a pained look, he answered, "He has temporarily left home to live with some relatives — my daughter has not been informed of this or where anyone else has been moved. You did the correct thing to leave — she is very distraught and not thinking straight."

Well, I figured there were worse places to be stuck. For a little while I just imagined I was on vacation in France, lounging around in a beautiful, colourful little oasis, a peaceful paradise far away from any danger. Of course I had to block out the sound of Ben's radio as he conferred with London about where we were and what our next op would be.

Ben looked up from his radio with a look on his face like a kid whose hockey team had just won the Stanley Cup. "It's started. The invasion. Normandy!"

I almost let out a whoop of joy but contented myself with shaking hands with everyone there. The rest of the day flew by as we discussed strategy and what they might be doing and how the battle might go.

Cary Grant's wife brought us a small supper of vegetable stew and fresh bread. As we ate, John told me how lucky we were to be fed so well, because the Germans had gutted the country, taking all the food and sending it to the Front for their soldiers or back to their homeland. Starvation or near starvation was everywhere. I hadn't understood that every bite we took was food right out of our hosts' own mouths.

Then, before I knew it, the boy — I knew his name was Michel because the girl had let it slip — arrived and told us he'd be taking us to the rendezvous, because he knew the area so well. As soon as it got dark enough we were going to collect a drop of supplies from the RAF.

Ben told Michel the coordinates of the drop and then we followed him, walking for almost an hour to a clearing in the woods. By the time we arrived at the rendezvous, the same men from the night before had constructed a makeshift landing strip using small fires. I hadn't been able to see it at all from the road, and I hoped the Germans couldn't see it either.

We heard the drone of a plane. I knew right away it was a Lysander, just from the sound, and sure enough it soon roared in for a perfect landing. The men rushed over to the plane, heaved a number of containers out and began lugging them into the woods. As I heard the engine rev up for takeoff I helped unpack one of the boxes. There were lots of guns. I was actually nervous about having to use one. It would be completely different from firing a Browning while in our kite. This time it would be up close, at a man I could actually see. I wondered if I would freeze up. Then there was another worry — though I'd had some basic training, I hoped I wouldn't shoot off my own foot or anything.

I thought we'd be going right back to the greenhouse but we didn't. We headed instead toward Raymonde's house, which I figured out because I had made sure to always keep a keen eye on where we were going, and I had a pretty good sense already of the countryside around. I caught up with John and asked him what was happening.

"Our worst fears — at least Raymonde's. His daughter, Marie-Claire, went to the local mayor to plead for her fiancé's life. The mayor turned her right over to the Germans and it wasn't long before she gave up her father and mother. Raymonde thinks the blasted Hun have sent her back home as *bait* in order to catch him. He wants help getting her away from the farm."

"But if we take her with us she'll just escape and hand us in," I protested.

"He thinks she must have learned the hard way that you can't trust the Hun. Anyway she's his daughter — he's not thinking clearly." He paused. "I figure we'd better help him. Others in the Resistance won't be as kind to her."

"They'd kill her?" I asked.

"In a minute," he answered. "About a week ago they caught a collaborator, beat him in front of the whole town, then executed him." He shrugged. "I wish I could have stopped them. Rather not see that again."

"But Raymonde got away," I said. "How?"

"He has a contact in the mayor's office," John answered. "The fellow managed to get word to Raymonde, but his wife was picked up in town before he could reach her. One of his sons is working in Germany — slave labour — and the other is off fighting with the Resistance somewhere. Right now Marie-Claire is the only family he has left."

I thought about the pale young girl only my age and how she probably was so desperate to save her fiancé that she'd put everyone else she loved at risk. Enough to break a person, I thought. How could you live with a choice like that?

"Hurry! Hurry!" I heard from Raymonde just ahead of us. I smelled the fire before I saw it. We reached the trees that edged his property and saw that the entire place was up in flames. Two Germans stood beside a big black car. In front of the farmhouse door stood Marie-Claire. She was screaming for help. But the Germans had guns pointed at her. They were going to force her to run into a bullet or burn alive!

Raymonde was about to rush ahead when John grabbed him and held him back. He told one of the other men to hold Raymonde there. Then quickly he gave everyone a job. Three of the men were to draw the enemy's fire from the trees just to the west. They moved off to take their positions. John and Ben would take the Germans down. I was to run to the house and rescue Marie-Claire. For a split second I wondered if she deserved to be rescued and why we were all risking our lives for a traitor.

"Want to end up like those blockheads?" Ben said to me, pointing at the Germans.

Shame washed over me. I knew right away what he meant. And I knew the answer. A young girl was about to die and we could save her. That was all there was to consider.

"No," I answered.

"Me neither," he said. "Let's get going."

Chapter Eight
June 6, 1944

Quick as I could I made my way along the trees
and got as close to the house as possible. I wasn't
quite set when a low whistle from John signalled
the others to begin. Gunfire erupted from the
trees. The Germans turned west to return fire. At
that moment I saw John and Ben step out from
behind the trees in order to get the best shots they
could, even though it made them easy targets
for the Germans' gunfire. I dashed out from the
bushes and ran straight for the house. I felt completely exposed — which I was. Marie-Claire had
stopped screaming and was watching, her back
against the door, unsure what was happening.

"Your father's waiting," I screamed to her.
"Viens ici! Viens ici!" I held out my hand to her
as I ran forward. Shots rang out but I had no idea
whether any of them were aimed at me or at her. I
kept running. *"Maintenant!!"* I screamed.

Finally she seemed to realize that this was her
only chance to escape and she staggered toward

me. She seemed too weak to run at speed — she might already be suffering from smoke inhalation, I thought. I'd sometimes gone with Pops on house calls to fires, and knew how easy it was to be overcome by the smoke and even to die from it before the flames ever got close enough to burn a person. She fell into my arms so I picked her up and carried her back to the trees. As soon as we had some cover I put her down. I could feel something wet as I did. Blood. Had she been shot? Had I? With all the adrenaline coursing through my body, I might not even feel it.

"Can you walk?" I asked her in French.

She was coughing but she managed a yes. I put her arm around my neck and half-carried, half-dragged her to the spot where we'd gathered before. Raymonde grabbed her from me and hugged her tight.

"I think she might be wounded," I cautioned.

The gunfire had stopped. Everyone else had made it back.

Ben nodded to me. "That's it for them," he said with satisfaction, clearly meaning that the Germans were dead.

"Let's get her back to the greenhouse," John said.

Raymonde and another of the men half-carried Marie-Claire as we hurried as fast as possible back to some sort of safety.

Ben walked beside me as we went. "We might need to move out of this area altogether now," he said. "The Krauts are nothing if not efficient. They'll flood this place with troops right away, looking for the fighters who did this. The green-house is quite a ways from the farmhouse, but probably not far enough. I bet there'll be a search of every single house in this area."

"And all the men they'll use for that won't be at the Front fighting our guys," I said.

I couldn't see his face in the dark, but I heard a smile in his voice.

"We might not be able to be at the Front or in the skies, but we're still doing what we can." He slapped me on the shoulder. "Good work tonight."

"I'm just glad I didn't have to use a gun," I confessed.

"I'm sure your buddies are too," he chuckled.

When we arrived at the greenhouse, Marie-Claire was gently settled on the floor. Her father tried to comfort her but had no idea what to do — and it seemed the others didn't either.

"May I have a look?" I asked.

I bent over her. She had been shot, all right. In the arm. From what I could tell it looked like the bullet had gone right through, so all that was needed was to stop the bleeding. I asked if we could get a clean cloth and some alcohol to clean the wound. Soon the man who owned the house appeared, along with his wife. She helped Marie-Claire up and declared that the girl would be spending the night in the house, not out here on a cold floor, and that she would tend to the girl's wound. John was about to object, worried for the older couple's safety, but shut his mouth when he saw the look on the woman's face. I suspected he knew when he was about to lose an argument.

Once Marie-Claire was taken away, we sat with Raymonde and the others and discussed what the next move should be. After some back and forth, the group decided to move farther south, away from this immediate area. Ben checked in with London and was told where we would be most useful.

"Let's be off, lads," John said.

It was around midnight. I began to think of sleep as something as precious as food, but something I'd be even less likely to get.

We followed Raymonde down a small country road. We could hear traffic on the main road — possibly the enemy was out looking for us already — as well as planes in the distance. More of ours, I hoped.

We walked all night. Just before dawn we arrived in a small village and there Raymonde split us up. Ben and John and I were taken to a house; the other men, he said, would go to a farm just on the outskirts. We were to meet that night in the woods due east.

John knocked at the door and a boy of about twelve opened it. He nodded and waved us in. His grandmother was already up, brewing the chicory they used instead of coffee. She motioned for us to sit at the table, as if this were an everyday occurrence. Maybe it was! We sat down and she fed us hot chicory and warm bread and butter and jam. I was starving and ate every last bite, even scooping up the crumbs with my fingers. Then she motioned for us to go into a back room, which was a bedroom with two twin beds. John and Ben took one look and each claimed a bed, just taking the time to remove their boots. That was seniority, I thought to myself, but I was so tired all I wanted to do was lie down. I collapsed onto the floor and was asleep in minutes.

Chapter Nine
June 7, 1944

Screams coming from the front of the cottage woke me. I looked around, groggy and not quite alert, when Ben hissed, "Grab your gun!" Then he strode over to the door, gun raised, John right behind him. Ben opened the door a crack and peeked out. He seemed to pause for a moment as if he couldn't believe what he was seeing, then shook his head and whispered, "The old girl is crazy!"

John pushed him aside to look. I could hear the boy yelling to his grandmother to be quiet. After a few moments she stopped and the young boy came into the back room. He was very apologetic.

"She hates the Boche," he said. "She can't help herself."

"She was yelling at the Boche?" I asked in disbelief.

"Yes," the boy said. "The good thing is, she does it all the time. Whenever they come into the village, she stands at the window and screams at them, and shakes her fists, so they don't pay her any mind. Maybe it's even safer here — they'd never imagine she would draw so much attention to herself if she were hiding the Resistance."

John laughed. "What a cover!"

We were invited into the front room to eat, the boy assuring us that the Boche had left. Soon a very pretty young woman appeared. She informed us that we were now on orders to disrupt the Boche's communications, so we'd be disabling telephone wires. She left to spread the word to the other Resistance groups, then came back to be our guide. Ben told me that it was often young women who were the couriers between various Resistance groups, because the Krauts found it harder to pin anything on them.

Our guide walked us through the fields and onto a narrow country lane. We travelled for a half-hour in a light drizzle, so by the time we reached the small clearing we were damp and cold. Still, all my discomfort was forgotten when I saw that we were joining a much larger group of about ten young men. Our guide murmured to me, "The Jewish Resistance." I was surprised that they had their own group, but when I thought about it, it made sense. Especially if what Max had told me had any truth to it — the Germans were out to hurt them and the best defence is always a good offence.

John had the details of the strike ordered by

London, so he briefed the leader of the other group. Raymonde and his men then made an appearance too. I could see that this was to be a very large operation. When the men had finished conferring, John told me and Ben that we'd be working with the Jewish group to cut the wires, while Raymonde and his men kept watch. I ended up walking along with a fellow about my age who spoke excellent English. I asked him how his group came about.

"My friends were all joining the Resistance," he said, "which was a good thing, so . . . "

"But you and your friends could only have been — what?" I interrupted, looking at him. "Fourteen or fifteen?"

"Hah!" he replied. "Many joined at thirteen! After all, as soon as the Germans marched into Paris they started passing anti-Jewish laws, first taking away the rights of Jews who were foreign nationals, then — "

Again, I interrupted. "What do you mean taking away rights?"

He looked at me as if I were some sort of idiot who knew nothing. "Rights. Citizenship! Jews became non-people and then they were sent to the camps. After the Germans finished with the foreign Jews, they started with the naturalized Jews. And not with the lesser known, you know, so people might not take notice. It's as if they wanted to shout it out: 'We can do whatever we want with you, and no one — especially your French brothers — will stop us.' How right they were."

He paused for a moment, so lost in thought I wasn't sure he was going to continue, but eventually he did.

"The Jewish judges and lawyers and business-men were taken first. And then the government started passing laws so that Jews were forbidden to go to a theatre or a restaurant or a swimming pool or a park. We could shop between three and four in the afternoon and we all had to wear a yellow star on our clothes."

"But why did anyone put up with it? I can tell you, if anyone had tried to do that at home — in Canada — we would have made their life a misery!"

"Really?" he said. "Then I wonder why your country won't take in any Jewish children with visas. We tried to get a large group out of a camp. They had visas for Canada, the Germans said they could go, and Canada refused to take them."

"I don't believe you!" I said. "We're here fight-ing *beside* you." I wanted to take a swipe at him. Everything he was saying seemed so crazy.

"I don't deny you are here and fighting and I'm pretty damn happy about that," he said. "But you asked why I joined a Jewish group instead of a regular group, and I'm trying to tell you. There are special reasons for us. We're always on the lookout, for instance, for Jewish children that can be saved or hidden."

"And have you been able to do that?" I asked.

"Yes, but the less you know about it the better," he said. "If you're ever caught, I don't need you spilling any secrets."

"I would never do that!" I protested.

"Anyone will if tortured long enough."

"Abe!" called their leader. "Up here."

He tipped his hat to me then and wished me luck.

The rest of the operation that night, I just did as I was told and tried not to get in anyone's way, but all I could think about was what Abe had told me. If it were true, I'd been living in some kind of dream world and things were so much worse than I could ever have imagined.

We had a couple of close calls with patrols. Abe and his fighters took out some Germans who got too close to us while I was atop a telephone pole! I was helpless up there and if they hadn't been such good shots I probably would have bought it right then. On the other hand, I got so good at scrambling up the telephone poles that by night's end I was nicknamed "*Grand Singe*."

Chapter Ten
June 29, 1944

It was a little after sunrise when the pretty girl, Louisa, came to the house quite breathless, and said, "We need to move you."

My heart sank. Grandmama and her grandson Alain had become like a second family to us. We ate with them, told stories to the young boy, who doted on every word and wished he were old enough to go with us every night as we cut telephone wires, blew up bridges and set explosives on rail lines. I felt safe here in a strange way, and didn't want to go anywhere — except straight back to England — and I doubted that was in the cards. We'd been at their house for weeks now and somehow I had got used to it.

"What's happened?" John asked.

"The Boche are doing a massive sweep in this area," Louisa said. "House by house. Ripping out floorboards, going into attics. They seem determined to find every last downed flyer and every last Resistance fighter."

"Desperation," John said, with satisfaction. "The Allies are getting closer and closer. The Hun can sense they're losing."

"Desperation or not," Louisa said, "you need to move."

She explained that they were going to try to send us on the escape line through Spain. I felt uneasy. At least we knew we could trust Grandmama and Louisa and Alain. But once we were sent along the escape line, who knew who we'd run into. I hoped at least I'd be able to stay with John and Ben. I didn't like the idea of being on my own again, perhaps wandering from stranger's house to stranger's house.

"Now!" she urged.

I think we had all assumed that we'd be waiting for nightfall, but she meant that we needed to go immediately! Ben ran and packed up his radio. I had nothing to pack except my small escape kit, which I quickly tucked into my jacket pocket — a jacket Louisa had given me, in fact, in exchange for my cable-knit sweater.

"You don't want anything on you that shows you're an RCAF airman," John instructed me.

On the other hand, I didn't want to leave my ID tags in the house to be discovered.

Louisa said, "Leave them. The boy will bury everything."

We went outside to find four bicycles waiting for us. "You'll follow me," she said.

And off we went in full daylight. But we didn't go down any main roads, instead sticking to back roads — which made for a very bumpy ride. My teeth were rattling and my head felt like it might shake off from my neck at any moment. But that was nothing compared to the feeling of being out in the open for anyone to see. I hoped we just looked like three ordinary farm workers. Luckily, we ran into no Germans, although we did pass some farmers who glanced at us and then quickly went back to work.

The day was becoming hotter and hotter and it must have been late morning by the time we pedalled up to a farmhouse near a small village. Suddenly it all seemed familiar to me and I realized it was the same village where I had met the young boy I now knew as Michel, who had sent me on my way that first day. And before I knew it we were driving up to his barn.

"Wait a minute," I called to Louisa. "I know this place. His sister is far too friendly with the Boche."

"You'll only be here one night," she said. "And this is the one place they won't search."

I supposed that might be true. Why should they

when one of their own could just walk into the barn and discover us!

The barn door opened and Michel stood there grinning. When he saw me his grin widened.

"Idiot!" he exclaimed.

Ben laughed. "Your reputation precedes you!"

"Very funny!" I said. "Can't say I like the idea of hiding in the place of a known collaborator."

The boy understood the word "collaborator" and spat, the same thing he'd done when first talking about his sister. "Francine is afraid now," he said in French. "She begs me for my protection when the Boche leave. I pretend I will help her. But there is no help for her once we have our country back."

I could see in his eyes that there would be no mercy for his sister, not even from her own family.

"Tomorrow after the Boche leave, a car will come and pick you up," he said. "You'll be driven into Paris."

At that Louisa wished us luck and got back on her bike. Michel closed the door but reappeared a short time later with lunch. Ben contacted London and, in a very quick transmission that he hoped wouldn't be traced, told them that we were on our way to the Comet Line, the code word for the Spanish route. Then he buried the radio in the hay at the back of the barn.

John had managed to pick up a deck of cards at some point over the last couple weeks and we spent the rest of the day playing poker, using hay as money. It passed the time and kept our minds off the uncertainty to come.

We all heard the German's car drive up to the farm just after dinner. To be on the safe side we retreated to the back of the barn, out of sight, just in case he did a cursory search. He didn't though. That didn't mean I slept well. I doubt any of us did. I lay there with my eyes open, my gun at the ready.

Chapter Eleven
June 30, 1944

I guess I drifted off again because I awoke with a start to the sound of a car's engine revving up. I gripped my gun so hard it's a miracle I didn't shoot someone by accident. But the car drove off and soon after, Michel arrived with break-fast. We'd just finished eating when another car arrived. It was a big black Opel like the ones the Nazis drove. We all piled into the back and then off we went.

Now I was even more nervous. Here we were in plain sight of the Germans. None of us had fake papers. No ID at all in fact. The driver was a middle-aged man who was well dressed but seemed to have little interest in talking to us — perhaps because he was very nervous too. I hoped that was the reason and that we hadn't just gotten into a car that was taking us right into the enemy's hands.

We finally drove off the small gravel road and onto the main highway. Immediately we encoun-tered the Germans — mostly trucks with soldiers standing up in the open cargo areas. Rows and rows of trucks as far as the eye could see. Anti-aircraft guns were positioned all along the road, just waiting for our fellows. It seemed they must be expecting an attack. And then we saw the Tiger tanks! I'd heard of them of course, these formidable weapons, but to see them this close was unbelievable! We could almost touch them! And by their black uniforms I could see the troops belonged to the Panzer divisions.

I couldn't understand why our driver was taking this route.

"I say, old boy," John said to the driver. "Do you really think this is wise?"

The fellow didn't reply so John repeated his question in French.

"No other way into the city," the driver replied. "Do they look interested in us?" he asked.

"Not especially," John answered.

"They aren't in the least," the fellow answered. "They're heading west to fight. They couldn't care less about a car with a few men in it. On the other hand, the Boche in the area we just left, the ones searching for Resistance fighters, they would be *very* interested. We have more to fear from a bombing raid courtesy of *your* fellows right now."

I supposed that was true. And not long after, I

did hear the drone of planes. Must be the Yanks, I thought. They did the daylight raids. I saw that Ben was thinking the same thing as I was when a slow grin lit up his face. He didn't care if we were caught in a raid — he just wanted these Germans stopped.

But before any bombs started to fall and the anti-aircraft fire began, we finally made it into Versailles. Not far from there we entered a suburb and came to an old stone house set in a few acres of land. A middle-aged woman met us at the door and ushered us in. It turned out to be the home of the driver of the car. I wondered how he had managed to get fuel and keep his car, and even how he'd kept the house out of the hands of the Germans.

I found out quickly.

"You have an urgent message from the hospital," his wife said.

He nodded. Then he turned around and left once again.

So he was most likely an important doctor, a surgeon even. Someone the Germans had more use for alive than dead. And in his spare time he helped out the Resistance. Or, I thought, he could be a collaborator and soon we'd be picked up by a few Gestapo agents. That thought made my blood run even colder than it had in the car.

But for the moment we were certainly treated well. His wife invited us to share a late dinner with her and then showed us to our rooms as if we were house guests. We were even each offered a bath! The water was lukewarm but the luxury of a bath was something I had not even dreamed of.

A bit later the doctor returned and offered us some red wine. John was very circumspect with his conversation, never really giving anything away, just talking in generalities about the war.

And for the first time since being shot down I slept in real bed. At first it felt so wonderful — the clean sheets bringing back memories of home — that I couldn't sleep. When I finally did, I dreamed of eating Mother's chocolate cake and of her hanging sheets out to dry in the backyard while the weeping birch swayed in the wind and the warm air surrounded me like a baby in a warm blanket.

Chapter Twelve
July 1, 1944

At breakfast, the doctor told us that it was too dangerous to keep us all together in one spot and we were to be separated. He would be taking me to a different safe house immediately. I didn't want to go off on my own. But I had no choice. We were at their mercy for good or ill and I had to hope it was for good.

John shook my hand and said, "Good luck, old chap."

Ben also shook my hand and, with a wink, said, "Take it easy, kid."

I saluted my two friends and left with the doctor.

He drove me right into the heart of Paris. I sat in the front seat with him this time. And perhaps I looked as miserable as I felt because he broke his stony silence and talked to me.

"You really are safer apart from each other," he said.

I nodded, but was still unconvinced.

"The Boche are getting more desperate, you see," he explained. "They know it's almost over. The dream of a thousand-year Reich will never happen. But they hope at least for good terms. They hope to salvage something."

"Or maybe," I said, "Hitler *doesn't* think it's over. And they are fighting so hard because he says they have to. Whenever I've seen him in the newsreels he looks crazy."

"Crazy?" The doctor thought for a moment. "All murderers are crazy," he agreed, "otherwise they couldn't murder. But clinically insane? I'm not so sure. And do not forget, Hitler is a murderer who has the support of millions. And there are so many who murder on his orders. Mass insanity? Perhaps. But I fear it is something much worse."

Now that he was talking he was really talking!

"What?" I asked, very curious.

"I suspect that Hitler has learned to prey on people's primal instinct — fear — and that even if we defeat *him* there will always be others who will do the same."

I really didn't know what to say. I don't think he actually expected an answer. It was almost as if he were thinking aloud.

"Yes," he said, "make people afraid enough and they will follow you and do almost anything."

"What were Germans so afraid of?" I asked.

The doctor shook his head. "That's the irony. They were afraid of the riots and the turmoil, the messiness of democracy. Hitler took a yearning for simplicity and order and turned it into a force that could not be stopped. It was easy, no? Orderly, no? No more mess. Democracy, my young friend, will always be at the mercy of those who say things run much easier and smoother without it! Just let us do our jobs, they say, without all this turmoil."

"But," I replied, "after this, if we win, who would say that?"

He glanced over at me then, and almost smiled. "Ah," he said, "to be young! Now, enough of my ramblings. Look about you. We are driving into Paris. When you get home you can tell your family about seeing the most beautiful city in the world."

We stopped outside a large apartment building on the Champs Élysées. The street was beautiful, broad and tree lined. The building we stopped at looked pretty grand. As I stepped out of the car, for one brief moment I felt like a tourist — until a German convoy drove past us and the doctor motioned me to hurry along. As he took me up four flights of stairs he told me that the plans had changed. We were not to be smuggled out through Spain, but taken to an airfield outside the city and picked up by a British plane. I wondered why we had to come into the city at all, but remembered that the countryside where we had been had become too dangerous. I was just relieved that there was a plan for us at all.

The doctor knocked three times on a door when we reached the fourth floor. I almost laughed. It really was like a Bogart movie.

There was an anxious couple of minutes before the door opened. When it did I couldn't believe my own eyes. Max! Max was standing there, leaning heavily on a cane. I almost toppled him when I grabbed him in a big bear hug. He returned the hug. Then we just stood there for a moment beaming at each other.

"Get in, get in," urged the doctor, looking nervously down the hallway.

I hurried inside and the doctor shut the door. "I see you two know each other," he said.

"We were in the same crew!" I exclaimed.

"Well, then, you won't be bored waiting for the next step," he said. "Someone will bring you food. Don't go outside for any reason — none. Do as you're instructed by whoever contacts you next. Someone else will be by eventually to take you to the rendezvous site." And before I could properly thank him he had left.

I quickly took in my surroundings. We were in a small flat with a window at the back of the building. There appeared to be at least one bed-room — and our own bathroom, which was good, as sharing one down the hall would only increase our chances of being caught.

I grinned at Max. "So? What happened to your leg?"

"Want the whole story?"

"I bet we'll have enough time for the whole story and thirty more like it," I said. "Looks like I'm stuck here with you for days!"

"Looks like that." Max grinned back. He settled down on the couch and I took a chair opposite. Slowly he raised his leg and put it up on the couch. He looked thin. The crew used to call us Mutt and Jeff. Where I'm tall, big and muscled, he's short, thin and wiry. Where I'm blond and blue-eyed — a Viking, according to him — he's got dark curly hair and brown eyes. So when we'd go to London on leave together you'd think I'd be the one to get the girls! But it was always the other way round. They'd crowd around Max as if he were a honey pot and they were the bees.

"Did anyone else make it?" I asked before he started.

"I know for sure that Stan and James made it,"

he said, "and now you and me. Well, that's four out of seven. I saw the two of them run for it, but they didn't see me and I didn't want to call to them and maybe alert the Germans. I broke my ankle when I hit the ground. I saw some other chutes too — so maybe everyone got out. But I also heard gunfire and wonder if the skipper got away in time or . . ."

I shook my head. "He didn't make it," I told him. "I was told they'd recovered two bodies. But Bill made it out and we stayed together until we found him a doctor and some help."

There was a pause for a moment as Max took that news in, both the good about Bill and the bad about Lew. It sounded like Phil must have been the other one who didn't make it. Still, five out of a crew of seven surviving a crash — I guess that was more than we could have hoped for.

Then I asked, "How on earth did you get away after breaking your ankle?"

"I knew I couldn't stay there so I just had to move. Wasn't pretty." He grimaced. "I basically crawled on all fours all that night and even then I only reached some woods by morning. The next night I crawled again. I found a stream, though, so that saved me. I decided to stay near the stream. On the third day an old granny saw me — she was out picking berries. She told me to stay put. Well, I didn't know if she would come back with the enemy or with the Resistance so I crawled again and tried to hide. Some men came that night but I was afraid to show myself. Anyway, the next morning I could see a farmhouse not too far away and that afternoon one of the farmer's sons came down to the stream for water. But I soon realized that he was looking for something — someone — and I figured I'd best take a chance. I can tell you that by then my ankle was throbbing and aching something fierce. So this boy helped me into the barn and called a doc and, you know, that doctor came every single day after he set my ankle and checked on me. And not long after, a few fellows from the Resistance showed up and I starting helping out, making bombs. Have you seen those little ones, like sausages?"

I nodded. "I made some too."

"So that was my job for weeks and then suddenly they said they had to move me and I got here just before you did! I was pretty nervous, I can tell you," he said. "Didn't know if this fellow was to be trusted. Talk about a cold fish."

"I had the same reaction when I first met him," I agreed, "but he grows on you."

"Tell me how you got here," he said.

I filled him in as briefly as I could about what had happened to me since the plane had been downed.

When I was finished he said, "So just showing off then, eh?"

I smiled. "Danes *never* show off," I said.

"Danish Canadians obviously do," he countered.

I paused before asking the next question. "Did anyone find out about . . . "

"Me being Jewish?" he said, finishing my sentence. "I decided that might be a good thing to keep to myself." He paused. "But you know how you feel like a fish in a fish pond just waiting to be scooped up?"

I nodded. "That's the way I've been feeling most of the time."

"I feel more like a walking target," he said, "with a big bull's eye on my back."

Chapter Thirteen
July 2, 1944

"Montreal smoked meat!" Max said.

"Danish meatballs!" I countered.

We had been occupying ourselves with the game, "Who makes better food, Danes or Jews?" for over an hour. We really shouldn't have been talking about food — it was just making us hungrier. There was no food in the apartment and no one had arrived with any.

"I thought maybe that doctor was going to take me straight to the Germans," Max said, finally changing the subject.

"I wondered too," I admitted, "until he started talking. No, I'm pretty sure he's okay."

And it was just then that we heard the three knocks on the door. My heart started pounding. Was this it? Were we going to the rendezvous already? And why was it always in broad daylight?

I went to the door and cautiously opened it a crack.

"The doctor sent us," said a lady, maybe in her

thirties. She had blond hair and wore a little black hat on her head. She slipped into the apartment. "Time to go."

There was no point in questioning her. How would we know whether she was on the up and up or not? And surely the only people who knew about us were the doctor and his contacts. . . . Of course I also knew that those contacts could go rotten at any point. Max and I exchanged a look.

"Both of us?" I asked.

"Oh yes, both," she answered. "Come now, we must hurry."

Maybe it was because she had knocked just when Max had been wondering whether or not we could trust the doctor, but I suddenly had a funny feeling in my gut. I looked at Max. He just shrugged. I'm not sure whether the shrug meant "What choice do we have?" or "I think she's okay." We only had two choices — go along or run for it. But how long could we last in Paris, with no papers? My French was passable and had certainly improved over the last few weeks. Max's was excellent since he was from Montreal, but his accent would certainly give him away.

We grabbed our jackets and followed her down the stairs. When we got to the street she told us to stick near her. She walked just ahead of us for a number of blocks and then turned into a small apartment building. She hurried up the stairs to the second floor and opened one of the doors. "I'll bring you some food later," she said. "Don't go out unless you need to use the loo, end of the corridor."

And she was gone.

"Whew," I said to Max. "I was suddenly sure she was going to turn us in!"

We looked around. It was a very small flat with an old couch, a rickety old chair and seemingly nothing else.

"Not exactly the Ritz," Max said.

I went to the small sink in the kitchen for some water, but there was none. "And no running water," I sighed. "We've certainly come down in the world, Max."

He sat down slowly on the couch and put up his leg.

"You kept up pretty well," I said to him.

"Not much choice," he replied, but I could see that now he was paying the price. His face looked a bit green.

It was hours later that the woman returned with a basket of bread, cheese and wine. She rushed off again before we could ask her anything.

"Have they never heard of water?" I said to Max grumpily as I drank some of the wine, which did very little for my thirst, as the day had just gotten hotter and hotter and the small room almost unbearable.

It was mid-afternoon when a knock at the door sounded and a different woman altogether came into the room. She was quite a bit older, stout and had a grim nod for both of us. "Come on," she said. "We're on our way out of the city."

Now this was the news we'd been waiting for! My spirits rose and I forgot all about being hot and tired and thirsty. I figured that maybe by tonight I could be back at base being debriefed.

I could see Max thought it was pretty swell too.

We followed her down the stairs into a waiting car. Our guide got into the front passenger side. A young man was driving but he had his cap pulled over his eyes and I couldn't get a clear view of him. The car screeched away from the curb and I thought that perhaps the driver could be a little more discreet, but he didn't seem to worry about that. In fact, he careened from street to street as if drunk, and that feeling I'd had in my gut earlier came back full force. This couldn't be right.

I had just had that thought when three large black cars pulled up around us. Our driver slammed on the brakes. A feeling of dread washed over me.

"We're for it," I murmured to Max.

Chapter Fourteen
July 2, 1944

The back doors were thrown open and I was roughly pulled out on my side as Max was on his. Two huge men patted me down and searched me while two others held machine guns on me. Of course I had no gun, no weapon of any kind — why were they so scared of me? What could I do to them?

They pushed Max and me back into the car. It jerked ahead again, except now the woman had a gun pointed at us.

"Traitors!" Max said in disgust.

She didn't answer.

"Where are we going?" I asked.

She didn't answer that either.

I felt so disappointed and so scared that for a moment tears burned at my eyes. And then I got mad. We had been *this* close to getting away . . .

Did the doctor know he had a breach in his cell — or worse, was he part of that breach? Somehow I still didn't think it was him. But now I wished

I'd listened to my gut. However, at least I'd had a chance to do some damage to the Germans before getting caught.

Max was silent. I'm sure he was wondering how long he could keep his secret. And would they even believe us when we told them we should be treated as prisoners of war? We had no identity tags. They could say we were spies and just have us shot.

It was a long drive. I don't think I really saw a thing as we moved through the city. Finally we entered a courtyard and the car stopped. Armed guards dragged us out of the car. I could see we were at a prison, a very large one. The windows were covered in heavy bars and more armed guards marched along the walkways above us.

"This is Fresnes Prison, I bet," Max said quietly to me.

The words were barely out of his mouth when the guard standing beside him hit him on the back of the head with his rifle butt. Max lurched forward. I managed to catch him before he fell. Then both of us were pushed from behind. One of the guards yanked open a huge steel door and then we were inside. A small entry gave way to another steel door. When that one slammed shut behind us I was quite sure there would be no escape from this place.

We were marched up a flight of stairs into a small room with only one chair and a small desk. An empty chair. The guards stayed with us, guns trained on us at all times. I glanced over at Max. His head was bleeding.

A Gestapo agent sauntered into the room and sat down behind the desk. He looked at me. Then he spoke in English. Quite perfect English.

"Name?"

"Sam Frederiksen."

"Rank?"

"Sergeant."

"Serial number? Service number?"

I gave him my service number.

"Place of birth?"

"According to the Geneva Convention governing captured prisoners," I said, "I am only required to give you my name, rank and service number, all of which I have done."

"Squadron number?"

"According to the Geneva Convention," I repeated, "I am only required to give you my name, rank and service number."

One of the guards jabbed me so hard in the lower back, just over my kidneys, that I fell forward. Max made a grab for me but I waved him away.

The guard came in front of me then and hit me so hard across the face that I reeled away in the other direction toward the door. "You'll be dead soon anyway," he growled, "so it doesn't matter."

Then they turned their attention to Max. He got the same questions and gave them the same answers.

"You've been working with the Resistance," the Gestapo agent said quietly. He had a long face and a hawk nose and a perfect English accent. I suspected he was not German, but had no idea what his nationality was — perhaps French? And perhaps someone who had attended Oxford or Cambridge, because his accent was very like John's.

"I was shot down over France and have tried to evade capture as per my orders," I countered. I suddenly realized that if I admitted we had anything to do with the Resistance I'd be shot! I'd lose my status as a POW. Max took my lead and repeated what I had said.

"Bridges blown up, rail yards, roads, you know nothing of this?"

"Nothing," I replied. And then I added, "And from now on I will only give you my name, rank and service number." I said that because I remembered in our briefings we were told that if we were captured, not to get tangled up in trying to be clever during an interrogation. The interrogators were experts at getting information, even information you didn't realize you might be giving away. Best to stick to the basics.

The man behind the desk then said, "We want to know how you got to Paris. Just tell us that and we won't bother asking you about anything else."

So they didn't know about the doctor! I vowed right then that I would die before I gave him away. And I gave them my name, my rank and my service number.

Chapter Fifteen
July 2, 1944

A guard knocked Max's cane out from under him and forced him to stand straight on his bad leg. Whenever Max faltered the guard hit Max's leg with the butt of his gun. But Max just picked himself up, stood up straight and stared at the man behind the desk.

The Gestapo agent asked me and Max the same questions over and over and we each gave the same answer over and over and in between we were hit or punched. I started to lose track of time. My main reaction, outside of the pain, was disbelief. We were prisoners of war, after all. We were flyers. How on earth could they justify treating us in this brutal manner? I'm not even sure I really felt the pain, in fact, I was just so shocked.

Finally the Gestapo agent nodded to the guards and we were led away, Max without his cane and compass, both of us without our watches and our jackets. We were marched through corridor after long corridor and steel door after steel door until we were put into a cell with two other men. Both were French — one very young, perhaps my age, the other quite old, maybe in his sixties. The older one looked rough. His face was a mess of dried blood and he was hunched over in pain. The younger one, seeing my reaction to the state of the older fellow, said, "He's just returned from his daily interrogation. He gets taken over to Gestapo headquarters every day. My turn tomorrow, I think."

I introduced myself and Max but our two roommates didn't seem inclined to tell us much. I guessed why immediately. They might think we were spies. So Max and I huddled together and tried to figure out what had happened.

"Obviously a serious breach in the Resistance," he said.

"But probably not the good doctor," I replied.

"Probably not," Max agreed. "I suppose we'll never know for sure." He paused. "I think it was the last lot. The first woman seemed okay to me, and she must be a more direct contact of the doctor. I bet it was the last two who turned us in — and if they keep doing that, no one will ever be able to tell the doctor his contacts are compromised, and he'll keep sending people right into the Nazis' hands."

"But I bet he has other routes," I said. "Maybe Ben and John went another way altogether. In fact, maybe that's why the doctor split us up — he suspected there was a breach somewhere. I mean, when we don't turn up for the flight it's bound to get back to him, right? Then he'll know something is up."

Max sighed. "Doesn't look like there's any way out of here. I just hope we'll be on our way to a POW camp today or tomorrow."

Only minutes after Max said that, another team of guards opened the cell door, took us out and marched us through still more corridors. We entered a large room. At the front of it were many tables, and seated behind the tables were men with mounds of papers surrounding them. I was pushed into a small cubicle at the back of the room and locked up. As I sat there I suddenly felt the pain of the interrogation. My face started to burn. My lower back, where I'd been punched, started to ache. I was thirsty and hungry and felt sick all at the same time. I wondered if I was going to throw up and if so, whether anyone would let me out of the tiny cubicle. I had a pretty strong hunch that they wouldn't so I took lots of deep breaths — my mom's recipe for avoiding vomiting. It worked, and by the time I was let out of the cell and marched up to the desk I was feeling a bit less woozy.

"Name."

I gave my name. And my rank and my service number and that seemed to be all the fellow wanted. I saw Max being shoved toward a desk as I was pushed by a guard and marched out of the room. I was taken through more hallways. After a very long walk I was thrown into a tiny cell, empty of anyone else, and the door was slammed shut behind me. The walls were a dirty white. There was a small table and chair and a cot, all bolted into the floor, and a toilet in the corner, but there was no washstand or other running water. At the end of the cell was a window. It was barred, and on the inside of the bars was frosted glass. Quickly I checked the door to hear if there was anyone outside the cell. The door had a peephole, but only so they could see in, not so I could see out. It sounded all clear.

The glass was framed with putty. The only moveable objects in the room were a spoon and a bowl. I pried away at the putty using the spoon until the frosted piece finally came out. Heaven! Fresh air flowed in. And on top of that I could hear voices! Men and women calling to each other!

I peered out the window. I was on the ground

floor and could ony see a courtyard, empty at present, and on the other side the high walls and windows of the prison.

I tried to catch what the voices were saying. Much of it was in French but I heard some English right off the bat. "A cobra is a deadly snake." Then laughter. The voice was American. Was that a code name for a new offensive? I hoped so. The rumour was that Canadians were taking heavy casualties in and around Caen. I heard men shout their names and then others shout back if they knew them.

I kept waiting for Max to be thrown in with me but that didn't happen. Finally I heard movement outside. Quickly I shut the window and sat on my bunk. The door didn't open, but a tray was pushed in through a narrow opening at the bottom. The only thing on the tray was a small bowl of fake coffee. No bread, no water, no anything!

I slurped it up and after a while there was a rap on the door and the clattering of a cart. I put the bowl back on the tray and shoved it through the slit. I suppose that was correct because I heard nothing after that.

I went back to the window then and opened it up. I heard men shout their names and others shout back if they recognized them. That's when I heard, "Max from Canada."

I yelled out, "Sam from Canada!"

"You okay?" Max yelled.

"Sure!" I yelled back. "You?"

"Never better!" he yelled.

And then others took up the messages and the banter.

It was getting dark and it had been a long day. I was aching all over. And thirsty. The fact that I wasn't hungry at all said everything about the shape I was in.

I thought maybe it was time to lie down. I looked warily at the bed, wondering if there were lice and such in the mattress. After all, there was no running water, there was no way to stay clean. Probably the bed was the dirtiest place in the cell. I decided not to risk it. When I was in Grade Five, head lice had gone around my school. What a nightmare. I thought I would scratch my head off. I certainly didn't want to get infested — and these were the only clothes I had too. So I decided that the cold floor would probably be a better choice than the mattress. But the floor was so cold that after about a half hour I was chilled through. So I sat on the chair with my legs up on the table and drifted off that way.

I don't know how long I'd been asleep when I woke with a start and cried out in pain. I had the most awful cramp in my calf. I leaped up and for a moment I didn't know where I was. I felt a fear so deep and so intense I cried out. After a few moments I came to myself. And then I heard the knocking through the wall in Morse code.

"All right?"

"All right," I answered back.

But I wasn't. Would I be dragged out for interrogation at any minute? How much pain could I endure? What would they do to me? It was said that every man had a breaking point. What would mine be?

Finally morning dawned and with relief I realized that I had made it through my first night with no one coming for me and with no torture.

A tray was passed through to me. It was the same meal as the night before — fake coffee and nothing else. And then the day began to drag along. I could only live in dread of being tortured for so long. I needed to take my mind off it, so I decided to do something with my time. After all, what if they actually did beat me to death or simply shot me? No one would ever know what had happened to me.

I noticed that there was an old rusty nail in the corner of the cell. I decided to use it to carve a message in the wall beside the bed.

I had just finished my masterpiece when lunch arrived. It was a small bowl of something — some sort of soup, which tasted like water, and a piece of black bread. I ate it in practically one gulp. I wondered if they would just starve us all to death. It occurred to me that being this hungry was actually painful. It hurt. Of course everything hurt — and sleeping that way hadn't helped. I wondered if I would need to take a chance on the mattress after all.

I paced up and down the little cell . . . up and down . . . up and down. Surely they would move me soon. I decided to throw the question out to the rest.

I shouted out the window. "Are they taking us to POW camps? Anyone know?"

"We see fellows taken away," someone shouted, "but no idea where to. We hear shots. Could be taken to firing squads."

I wished I hadn't asked.

I paced again. I definitely needed to take my mind off all this. I thought about my father's anatomy book I'd been studying. I decided to see if I could name all the body parts — or how many I could name. I thought I'd start with skeletal and then go to muscular.

And after that I could try to name all the players on every single NHL team.

But before I forgot, I needed to mark the date. I needed to keep track of the time somehow. Underneath my name I placed a scratch with the nail and put a line through it and then another, since this was my second day.

I peered out the window. The day was grey and there was a light rain falling. It reminded me of my very first operation with my crew in *H Hall*. The weather had been exactly like this that day, and I remember tilting my face into the rain while I waited on the tarmac. I remember wondering if that would be the last time I would feel the rain on my cheeks. I had pictured dying in a flaming wreck, but I never pictured this!

We had flown to France on that first operation and encountered no problems until we dropped our load, but fighters were all around us. And that's when a Halifax, trying to avoid a fighter on its tail, dipped and pitched and ended up underneath us and then rose right under us and into us. Boy oh boy, when I saw it coming up toward us I figured we were done, but it just kind of bumped us right under my turret and then dove again.

Skipper wasn't sure what damage had been done to *H Hall* but he knew we couldn't land at Skipton when we got back. We couldn't take the chance that we were going to crash, and runways had to be kept clear, so we landed at Woodbridge and taxied in right past a Halifax that was in flames. We learned right afterward that the whole crew of the Halifax had made it out, and sure enough, it was the same plane that had nipped us. The thing I remember most about the whole thing was how calm Lew was the whole time and how it made the rest of us calm too. Lew. If I wasn't careful I was going to start to cry. Well, why not? No one could see me or hear me. So I did. I had a good bawl and actually felt a bit better after.

As I breathed in the smell of the fresh rain I thought, "One day I'll stand in the rain a free man." It wasn't so much a prayer, because my father didn't believe in any of that and brought us up the same way. But it was definitely a wish. And just in case my father was wrong, I said a short prayer. "If you do exist, God, I'd love a little help."

I figured it wouldn't hurt to ask.

Chapter Sixteen
August 15, 1944

I had just finished marking off the date — 44 marks, which made it August 15 — when my cell door opened and I was ordered out the door. I felt a wash of mixed emotions. I was thrilled just to be out of that cell. I'd gone over all my anatomy charts in my head, the NHL lists, every song I could remember, done multiplication in my head, division, calculus even. I'd pretended to eat every single meal my mom ever cooked for me — but that became too painful so I stopped that game. I listed all the girls I'd liked over the last three years and made imaginary columns of good traits and bad and then had given each a score. The best part of my days, though, was listening and participating in the chatter. Mostly it was rumours that every day got more and more hopeful. The Allies were getting closer and closer to Paris and then soon we'd be free. Sometimes it was arguments over base-ball teams or hockey players, and those were great too. But we had only so much energy for yelling back and forth, and often there was just silence.

I'd look out the window at the concrete and try to imagine what I would do the day I got back to England. And the day I got back to Winnipeg. I had to stop those daydreams though, because they all seemed to be about food. Being alone was the worst thing I think I'd ever experienced.

So when they took me out of the cell, somewhere in my mind I knew I might be going to a firing squad, but I almost didn't care. When they pushed me into a large cell with four others, I almost cried like a baby — especially when right away I saw that one of them was Max! I grabbed him in a huge hug until he almost had to push me off. "Where have you been hiding?" he asked.

"All alone in a cell," I replied. "What about you?"

"Right here. Allow me to introduce," he said, nodding toward the other three men in the cell. "Lester Wiebe, also RCAF."

We shook hands. "Just call me Les," the fellow said. I was pretty sure I recognized him from the Mess back at Skipton.

"Trent Fox, RCAF," Max continued.

I did know Trent. He was from Calgary. "How are you?" I asked.

He shrugged. "Seeing you must mean that things are changing — but for better or for worse, we don't know."

"Louis Meyer," Max said, and then muttered, "Jewish and a Frenchman too."

I nodded and shook his hand. He was a thin tall man in his twenties. His face was puffed up black and blue.

"I see they're treating you well."

"Well as can be expected," he answered in French. "At least I'm still alive."

"And finally . . . " Max said, and from behind Trent, James, our wireless operator, stepped out!

I couldn't believe my eyes and ended up giving him a big hug too.

"Don't know why you're so happy to see me," he complained. "I'm stuck in this rotten place with you!"

James was a character. He had been studying English at the University of Toronto before he'd signed up and he always had a quote to throw into the conversation, or some interesting story about Oscar Wilde. I remember when I first met him he said to me, "I suppose you're familiar with the most famous playwright of our day, George Bernard Shaw, who wrote *Arms and the Man*?"

"Yes," I said, "I studied him at school."

"Did you know," he replied, "that he is working on a sequel called *Legs and a Woman*?"

I smiled as I thought of that and grinned at him.

"James, I'm certainly not happy about you being stuck here," I said. "Not at all. But I'm very happy you're alive! What happened to you after we were shot down?"

"This and that," he said.

And suddenly I realized that although the fellow called Louis was probably just who he said he was, none of us could openly admit to being with the Resistance, just in case there was a plant listening. Or in case someone was tortured and then gave us away.

"There's a lot of that going around," I answered him.

I turned to Max. "So you've been here the whole time," I said, just confirming what I already knew from our shouts back and forth to each other.

Max nodded grimly. "We've had the privilege of being in a cell next to one where they've been torturing both men and women. We hear them scream morning, noon and night. Every day they've taken each of us out for 'questioning.'"

That's when I looked at them more closely. They all looked bad. Max had bruises on his arms and I could see now that all the men were bruised and probably black and blue under their clothes.

I shook my head. What could you say? I

wondered why they had been treated like that and I had been left alone.

"Have you heard the news?" Max asked.

I knew what he meant right away. I'd heard the news too, called out over the yard from cell to cell.

"The Allies are about to surround Paris," I said.

"And soon we will be liberated," said Louis with feeling.

"Where does all this information come from?" I asked.

"Some from the French guards," Louis said. "But we have friends who know the tunnels underneath this prison. They get in just long enough to tell us the latest and then they get out."

"And what's the scuttlebutt on what's going to happen to us?" I asked, thinking that it certainly didn't sound like Louis was a spy.

"That's all we've been discussing," James said. "Trouble is, the Germans won't want to just leave us behind so we can be freed to fight against them. Seems there's quite a lot of airmen stuck here as well as Resistance fighters," he explained. "This prison can hold thousands — Louis here says perhaps there are as many as thirty-five hundred prisoners in here right now.

"So, that leaves two possibilities. Either they shoot us and that takes care of that, or they take us out of here and ship us east into Germany. But can they spare enough men to do that?"

"See, we've already fulfilled part of our job," said Max. "After all, every man they use to guard us is one less that goes to the Front."

"In which case, if I were them I'd shoot us," I said.

"Ah, but there's one problem with that," said James. "I think they know they're going to lose. And if they shoot such a lot of prisoners with so many witnesses, they will certainly be found guilty of a terrible crime. Or if they try to shoot so many in the Resistance, maybe the city will rise up against them."

"Hah!" exclaimed Louis. "As if those cretins care about that!"

"Maybe some do and some don't," said James. "At any rate, I suspect we'll find out soon enough. There may not be much time left before Paris is taken from them."

Shortly after that we were given our so-called lunch, and a bit later the door to the cell was thrown open and we were told it was time to go. We straggled out, hoping for the best.

We were led back through more corridors and one steel door after another, through the inner courtyard that had been my "view" and finally into the outer courtyard where we'd first arrived. There were already at least a hundred men standing there and a large group of women was herded in behind us. We were watched over not by the soldiers who had been guarding us, but by a new group in grey uniforms with what looked like side-by-side lightning bolts stitched onto their collars — SS! They carried machine guns over their shoulders, grenades on their belts, pistols in their holsters. Most of them were under thirty, fit and mean-looking. They shoved the women in behind us with no mercy and then made us stand there as the courtyard filled up with more and more prisoners, until there were at least a few hundred and more coming in every minute.

Max was beside me the whole time. We made sure to stick close together, along with James and the others.

"At least they aren't going to shoot us," said Max. "Way too many here for that."

"So?" I said. "Are we headed to Germany?"

"I'll never make it out of Germany alive," Max whispered to me. "I'll have to try to escape."

"I'm with you," I said.

Chapter Seventeen
August 15, 1944

We were put on a bus and driven through the city with a young Gestapo officer as our "tour guide." If it hadn't been so clearly sickening, I think I would have laughed. He talked away, showing us the sites, with no idea how disgusting it was for us to listen to him gab on as if he and his gang owned the city and could talk about it as if they belonged there and weren't occupiers and thugs! And this just after telling us — with a smile — that if anyone tried to escape they would be shot on the spot. I reminded him that we were RCAF flyers and should be treated as such, and he just said, "You are sounding very foolish. You were in a prison with Resistance fighters, therefore you are Resistance fighters and we are treating you exactly the way we treat them."

Max and I exchanged glances then, and my heart sank. Did that mean we were not on our way to a POW camp? That's what we had been hoping for, after all. That's the way we *should* be treated, no matter how we were caught or what their suspicions. We were still flyers! I looked at the Gestapo officer and his steely demeanour and was sure that he had no mercy in him at all.

We were lucky, I suppose, to be on a bus. The rest of the transport consisted mostly of large trucks with no windows, so those men had no idea where they were headed. I followed where we were going quite closely and figured we were moving into the eastern part of Paris, and then we were driven into a rail yard, a very large rail yard. We pulled up along a siding and were yelled at to *"Raus! Raus!"* which by then I knew meant "Get out." In front of us were cattle cars — not passenger trains but cattle cars! On the outside of each one was written *40 Hommes – 8 Chevaux.* They were small old boxcars made of wood. The sinking sensation I'd felt when the SS guard said we were to be treated the same as the Resistance got worse when the Germans screamed at us to get in. For a moment I wondered whether or not I should step up and demand we be treated with the respect we deserved, but those guards looked positively crazed, screaming and yelling at everyone, and by then there must have been the entire prison emptying out onto the siding.

That's when I heard it. The sound of thunder.

I looked at the sky. It was around midday by then and I couldn't see a cloud anywhere. In fact it was getting hotter by the minute. That sound could be only one thing then. Artillery fire! That's how close the Allies were! No wonder the Germans were so frantic to get us away. I suppose we were lucky they hadn't just shot us.

I noticed the Germans starting to swing themselves up into the boxcars on either side of us. Max and I were two of the last to be shoved into the cattle car and I swear there must have been almost a hundred men in there already. It was so packed that once in we couldn't move from our spot near the door and almost fell out again. And then the huge door was pulled shut and bolted and immediately it felt like there was no air at all. So many unwashed bodies in such close quarters.

It wasn't long afterward that the train started with a jolt and everyone fell against everyone else. I said I was sorry to a poor fellow whose toe I stepped on and then realized it was James when he said, "'I could be bounded in a nutshell and count myself a king of infinite space, were it not that I have bad dreams.'"

Despite the terror of what was happening, I had to smile. I remembered that quote from *Hamlet* when we'd studied it at school. And for one split second I was back at St. John's High, sitting at my desk behind Sadie Kobrinsky, her dark hair curling down her back, and me wondering if I had any chance at all of her saying yes if I asked her to go skating with me over the weekend. And how she had said yes, and less than two years later when she heard I was going overseas, she came to the house and kissed me right on the lips and wished me good luck. Right then I decided that if I made it home I was going to look up Sadie and see if she was free for a skate on the river.

The train jolted again, this time coming to a stop. And then it started again. I was taller than most and could see over everyone's heads. There was a bit of air coming in from windows beside the doors on either side. I suppose you could call them windows. They were really rough openings covered by steel bars and barbed wire. Still, at least some air got through — not enough to kill the smell, but enough to keep us alive.

It was barely possible to sit, let alone lie down, but at first there was lively chatter as friends who hadn't seen each other in weeks or months got caught up on what had happened to them, how they had been betrayed, or what had happened in Fresnes. But as the day wore on the chatter wound down. The ride started to take on the feel of a waking nightmare. For a bathroom there was one bucket at the end of the car and soon the smell was overwhelming — and when anyone had to get there it was almost impossible to move through the packed bodies. I was so tired that at times I almost fell asleep standing right there, but was always jostled awake by another stop or start.

"It must be all that bridge and rail work we did," Max said proudly. "We've blown up so much they can hardly make any headway."

I was pretty sure he was right. We were going so slowly, in fact, I wondered if there was someone walking ahead of the train looking for missing tracks or blown-up sections. That speculation turned out to be justified when the train screeched to a halt in a tunnel and didn't start up again. Smoke from the engine started to fill up the car. I began to cough. So did everyone around me. As the air became more difficult to breathe I started to panic and wondered if we would all suffocate right there and then. The air turned black. Tears streamed down my face. It occurred to me that we should get low, the way you do in a fire, but there was no room to sit. There seemed nothing to do but bang on the doors and yell for them to be opened, which those of us close enough to the doors did.

Finally, well over an hour later, the doors were thrown open and we were screamed at to get out. We staggered onto the dirt track, still in the dark tunnel, gasping for air.

"*Raus! Raus!*"

"I'll *raus* them," I muttered.

The guards grabbed their kit from their box-cars and gave it to us to carry. I had to shoulder a bag that must have weighed 50 pounds, as did Max. James was pushed to an outside line and in English we were told that if anyone tried to escape, those on the outside line would be shot first. And then we started to walk.

In a few minutes we were out of the tunnel and could see that we were in the countryside with a river on one side and above us, hills. People were riding bikes along our route. I suspected they were Resistance fighters — especially since many were women and I thought they might be looking for relatives in the group. That's when Max whispered to me, "I heard that the head of the Paris Resistance was in Fresnes when we were. Maybe he's on this transport. Maybe the Resistance is going to try to free us."

"If that means we don't have to go back into those trains again I'd risk anything," I said. "Even a firefight."

"Quiet!" screamed a guard.

They loved to scream. I wanted to tell them they sounded like little children with all their screaming — Allied servicemen would never stoop so low — but I decided to keep my mouth shut.

It was a long walk and I was getting weak from the lack of food and the heat and the coughing that still racked my body. When we finally reached a town and another train station and saw another train waiting for us, it turned out to be more cattle cars. I wasn't sure I could get inside one of them again, but what choice did I have? If I ran for it, even if I made it, someone else would die for me.

But that's when I saw something I hadn't expected. On the platform was a small group of women wearing Red Cross armbands. They were giving out both food and water. I was handed a piece of bread with some jam on it, and water to drink. It was great — even if the bread tasted more like sawdust than actual bread. And the water really helped calm down my cough.

I looked up to the hills. Quite a lot of locals were standing there watching us, but we were shoved back into the cattle cars, so it seemed that there was to be no rescue. Had the Resistance not been able to muster enough men that fast? I suspected that was the case. After all, we were guarded by elite troops, and lots of them. What would be the point of a bloodbath?

The day dragged on as the train stopped and started. As night drew on James told me that he'd had an idea. He suggested that if everyone sat with their knees up we might all be able to sleep. Since I was one of the tallest I was best able to convey the message, so I yelled at the top of my voice and we got a very good response. Soon everyone was seated and we did manage to finally get some sleep.

Chapter Eighteen
August 16, 1944

By morning nothing had changed. We received no food until late in the day. When the train stopped and the doors were finally opened we saw the Red Cross on the platform again. This time we weren't allowed out. Food and water was passed in to us. The water came in a large metal can and we had to pass it from person to person until everyone had a drink. But when it came back empty a Frenchman near me grabbed it and then crouched down with it. Intrigued, I bent over to see what he was going to do. He took the metal top and used it to lever up the nails that were holding down the wooden planks on the floor of the car. That's when the guards started calling for the water, which was okay because the fellow was done. There was a plank that was now off, but could be put back as needed, so if the guards checked from below it would look like the plank was in place. We passed the can back out and then the guards shut the doors.

A group of Resistance fighters had gathered

together and had begun to discuss the best way to use the escape hatch.

"We need to be careful about when to go," one said. "If we jump when the train is stopped they'll catch us. If the train is going too fast, we die. It needs to be just as the train is picking up steam, leaving the station."

"Can we send one of ours?" I asked the fellow who had just spoken.

He consulted with his friends and then said, "First five of us go, then you can choose five, then us five and so on."

I turned to Max. "You need to be the first of us."

He nodded.

My heart was pounding as we waited to get to another station and the first escape.

It was full dark when the train screeched to a halt. We were stopped for a few minutes, which felt like hours to me, the Frenchman poised over the opening on the floor. Finally the train lurched forward. The man waited about a half minute and then dropped. He was gone. We replaced the plank.

The train picked up too much speed right after the drop for anyone else to attempt an escape. So we waited. But happily we didn't come to a screeching halt followed by rapid gunfire! I hoped that the fellow had made a successful escape.

It was hours later before our next stop. Every minute seemed like an age to me, especially because there were many others in the line ahead of Max and then, hopefully, me. Most of the men in the car didn't even realize what was happening, which was just as well, I thought, since the lineup would be immense and fights might even break out about who was to go next. Although we had all followed the same pattern as the night before, sitting with knees up, those of us around the escape hatch, by staying low and just shuffling positions with each other, managed to keep what was happening secret.

The train started to slow and came to another stop. The second Frenchman got into place and we took the plank off for him. We were stopped for about ten minutes and then started again. He waited until we had picked up some speed and then he dropped through.

Three more went with no problem as the night wore on, and finally it was Max's turn. The train was stopped, Max was poised and ready to go when flashlights combed the outside of our car, the light beaming through the windows near the two doors on either side. This went on for a few minutes.

"Do you think they found the last guy?" I asked James, who was in line to go after me.

"No chance," he replied. "They'd be tearing apart the cars if they had. But maybe they noticed something — a shadow — and they didn't know whether it was a man or an animal or a tree . . . "

"Should we keep going?" I asked.

"I'm going," Max said. "It's my only chance. Otherwise I'm a dead man."

I certainly wasn't going to argue with him. He had to make that life-or-death decision himself.

Max shook my hand.

"I'll be right behind you," I assured him. "But don't wait around for me. Just get out of here and find our guys. And then do some damage to those Nazis."

"I'll do my best," he said.

The flashlights were turned off and shortly after, the train lurched forward.

"Ready?" I said.

"Ready!"

And then he was gone.

We put the plank back in place and I waited for my turn. I started thinking about what to do when I dropped. Should I stay on the track until the train was far away, or roll and run the minute it passed over me? From what I could see out our windows, every time the train stopped the SS dropped from their cars and surrounded each prisoner car so that no one could escape through a door or one of the windows. Then as the train started they grabbed the rails and leaped onto their cars. If they were looking back they might see me get up, so staying put until the train was out of sight would be the ticket.

And then I vowed to avoid all farmhouses, all help and to somehow make it to the Allied lines.

Finally the train came to a stop. And that's when someone near one of the windows called, "They're looking underneath the cars with flashlights!"

I looked at our plank. We'd be fine. It was in place and no daylight would show when they beamed their flashlights on it.

But then James said, "Sam. Sam! Look."

He was pointing to the edge of the plank. It was sticking slightly up.

"We need to take it out and put it back in again," I hissed.

"No," he said. "If they're underneath they'll see it right away. Press down on it, just try to push it back."

I pressed down on it and so did James and some others, most of us getting up, not caring who saw us at that point and practically jumping on it to make it fit back in properly.

Suddenly we heard, *"Ach! Ja!"* from below us.

"*For fanden,*" I swore.

"Damn and blast!" James echoed.

And then there was nothing left to do but wait.

Minutes later the door to our car was pushed open and about ten SS with machine guns pointed at us pushed us out of their way until they found the loose plank. They had brought boards and nails and within minutes they had put down a new plank. Then screaming words like *Schweinehund* and shoving their way through the men, they exited the car and rammed the doors shut behind them. We sat back down. I could hardly breathe, but whether that was from the fear of discovery or the horrible disappointment, I wasn't sure.

"Never mind," said James. "Another time."

I nodded, but couldn't even manage an answer, I was so overcome.

Chapter Nineteen
August 17, 1944

Morning came and went. We didn't stop at any more stations and were given no food or water. Finally — it must have been about noon — the train stopped and the doors opened. We weren't at a train station though. We were ordered out.

We straggled out, almost too stiff to manage the jump to the ground. Once we were all gathered in front of the boxcar, we could see that we were in the middle of a forest and that we were the only prisoners who had been "allowed" out. SS troops formed a line in front of us, then raised their submachine guns and pointed them at us.

This is it, I thought. Punishment for last night.

As if he could read my thoughts, James said, "It's our duty to escape. We have been ordered to try to escape at every opportunity despite the repercussions. Chin up. We die proud."

I stood straight then and thought, He's right. None of this is my fault. It's those Germans right there who started all this and none of us would be here if not for them. Damn it, but I'm not going to die shaking in my boots.

"Ausziehen! Ausziehen!" they started to scream at us.

One of our fellows called out, "They want us to take our clothes off."

For a moment no one complied. Then an SS guard shoved a man to the ground, kicked him and started pulling his jacket off.

So, reluctantly, we started to take our clothes off. Once we were down to our skivvies the guards kept yelling — they obviously wanted us naked. Now I was sure we were about to get shot, and instead of feeling embarrassed I got mad. Really, really mad. It wasn't enough for them to kill us, they had to humiliate us first.

I started to hum "You Are My Sunshine." My mom had sung that song while making dinner the last time I was home for leave before I shipped out. It made me think of home and family and love and hot food and cozy fires, and if these were my last moments, that's what I wanted to think about, not the hate-filled monsters in front of me. Somehow I felt my anger seep away and I stood there, naked like the rest, but ready.

And then something shocking happened. The

Germans ordered us back into the train. Still naked.

We scrambled back into the boxcar. Once we were inside they shut the doors and the train started up again. As before, we were stuffed together, but this time with no clothes. Now I *was* embarrassed! Still, there was nothing for it. Everyone started talking at once and soon the reason for the punishment made its way through the car until all the prisoners knew about the escapes. From what I could gather, most of the men were happy that at least some had got away, and didn't begrudge the attempt. It was our duty, after all, to make an escape if at all possible.

James and I were discussing all this when the unmistakable sound of a rifle shot ripped through the car just as the train came to another stop. The doors were opened and the guards once again pushed their way on board. It didn't take them long to find the person who had been shot. The word went through the car quickly. He'd been leaning up against the window, using the bar to hold himself up so he wouldn't bump into others — maybe he was more conscious of that now we were all naked — and the guards had seen his hand up against the opening and shot him! As he was dragged out past me I was sure I knew him.

And then it came to me. It was the young boy who had first called me an idiot. Michel! He was covered in dirt, his hair awry, and he was thin, as if he hadn't eaten in weeks. No wonder I hadn't recognized him earlier. He must have been swept up in the raids somehow and put in Fresnes prison as well. He was just a kid! How could they throw him in prison? And now what?

I squeezed myself in between the men to get to the opening of the cattle car and see what was happening to him. The guards yelled at him, accusing him of trying to escape. Because he had his hand on the window opening? Perhaps this was just another way to punish us or to demonstrate that no more escape attempts would be tolerated?

A guard ordered him to walk ahead. Maybe they were actually going to get him help for his injury. Everything was quiet. The forest even seemed still. No birds sang and no wind blew through the trees. It was as if the world held its breath.

I watched as the young boy, so thin I could have counted his ribs, staggered forward. And then the silence was shattered by machine-gun fire. Michel's arms flung out wildly and then he crumpled to the ground, shot in the back.

"You!" a voice said in English. A guard was pointing at me.

I pointed to myself.

"Yes, you. And beside you, that guy. Get down."

I leaped down onto the ground. James, who had been standing next to me, jumped down as well. I thought of taking a run at the guards, who stood with machine guns still raised — the murderers of a boy. I thought it would be worth it if I could take out one or two. But I knew that I'd be cut down before I took a step toward them.

I remembered that Max had told me the Germans were murdering Jews. I hadn't believed it. But what I'd just seen was evil in its purest form. And it made me feel something I'd never before felt. Despair. I despaired for the entire human race.

We stood there stark naked. One of the guards handed me a shovel and pointed to a spot beside the railroad track and motioned for me to dig. He did the same to James. We were to dig a grave.

I was surprised they were even bothering to bury Michel. I thought about his poor mother and how she would never even know what had happened to him. I wondered what had happened to his sister Francine, or what would happen to her after the war, and thought again about the mother whose daughter was a collaborator and whose missing son was a hero. I felt tears burning at my eyes, but didn't want to show any weakness to the Hun.

I was standing on wood chips and stones because we were near the tracks. Somewhere in my head I knew I was feeling pain and yet I wasn't really feeling it. I just dug and dug and then when there was a shallow grave the guard motioned for us to throw Michel in. Gently James and I picked up his bullet-riddled body and placed it in the ground. I wanted to say a prayer, but I didn't know any except the one we said in school, the Lord's Prayer, so I said that in my head as we began to cover the body with dirt. It was so quiet you could hear a pin drop. Not a sound came from the open car. Not a person spoke. The guards puffed away on cigarettes and sat on tree stumps as we worked.

And when we were done James murmured, "The rest is silence."

I put the shovel down on the ground, looked at James, and we walked back to the train car. We lifted ourselves in and shortly afterward the doors were yanked shut. The train started up.

Slowly the men started to talk again, more than likely about the murder they had just witnessed. I began to feel a stinging on my feet and looked down to see they were bleeding, as were James's. There was nothing to do about it though — we didn't even have clothes to use to wrap the wounds.

"The usual rules don't apply to these men," James said. "I doubt they've even been taught about the Geneva Convention, unless it was to be mocked as weak, something to ignore. If we cannot somehow become prisoners of the Luftwaffe, I fear for us all."

I could only nod in agreement. The train chugged along and we did stop finally for some bread and water and then somehow got into sitting positions for the night. That's when I noticed that the train was picking up speed. Somehow I just knew we had crossed the border and were out of France. And any chance for the Resistance to free us was gone.

I felt numb. Hungry and dirty and surrounded by the rank smell of unwashed bodies and the open-bucket latrine, I was lost in despair.

"They win if we give up," James said, sensing my mood.

"I know," I said. "But what does it say about the human race?"

"It says that we are capable of that kind of brutality — worse than animals, really, who don't kill out of malice. But we are also capable of great good and even heroism. 'What a piece of work is man!'"

"I suppose it would be easier," I said, "if I believed in God. I could believe that it was all His will and maybe I could accept it."

"I believe in God," said James, "and you know, it doesn't make this any easier. I just wonder how He could allow such things. But perhaps He doesn't get involved — just watches from on high and hopes for the best."

He thought for a moment. "I feel closest to Him when studying Shakespeare. When I see a spirit that can describe the human condition the way Shakespeare does, then I see God."

"Can you recite any of the speeches from his plays?" I asked.

"I know most of *Hamlet* by heart," he said.

"Really? Can you say it for me?"

"I can," he said, and he started to recite the play. Soon the men beside me stopped talking and started to listen, then the men beside them and the men beside them, until the entire car was transfixed.

We all listened more intently when he got to Hamlet's famous speech, "To be, or not to be: that is the question: Whether 'tis nobler in the mind to suffer the slings and arrows of outrageous fortune, Or to take arms against a sea of troubles, and by opposing end them?"

I'd always wondered about that speech, so I asked, "Does that mean to kill yourself?"

"Well, that's where the debate begins," James said. "I personally don't believe this is only, or even, about suicide, but about how we approach life. What happens when you take arms against a sea? Isn't that hopeless? But even if it is, perhaps what's important is the effort? We need to try."

"But doesn't he go on to say that he fears death more than he fears life?" someone piped up.

"Well, yes," James agreed and then went on with his recitation, but with many interruptions as we stopped to discuss the words and the meaning.

It was such a welcome break in the horror — I might have gone crazy if he hadn't taken my mind off things in that way.

Chapter Twenty
August 20, 1944

It was the sixth day when the train stopped at a station and someone peered out the window and called out, "Weimar."

Suddenly the door was opened and our clothes were tossed into the car. It took quite a while to find whose clothes were whose, but we finally sorted out one filthy pair of pants from another and most of us got our own clothes and got dressed. I began to hope that we were on our way to a POW camp and that they didn't want us to arrive naked — a clear violation of the Geneva Convention. We peered out the windows and saw a barbed-wire fence with men behind it dressed in blue and white striped pyjamas. They were surrounded by guards and looked so emaciated that I was amazed that they could even stand. I remember being told of millions of French men who had been dragged into Germany as slave labour and I wondered if that was what we were seeing and if these men would be able to hold on a little while longer until the war was over.

The train started again and chugged slowly up a hill. About a half-hour later we stopped and the doors were opened. We were herded out of the train, thousands of us, it seemed. We stood together just outside the main gate to — where?

In front of us was a high barbed-wire fence. Guards were screaming orders and dogs on leashes were snarling at us. Inside the gates I saw more prisoners in striped pyjamas, so emaciated they were little more than skeletons. What was even more disturbing was that they didn't seem to notice or care that a new group had arrived. They hardly glanced at us, and when they did their eyes looked dull and devoid of any curiosity at all.

There were guard towers spaced about a hundred yards apart, and behind us I saw woods filled with SS and their dogs, leading men in pyjamas — perhaps work parties? How would we ever escape from here? It looked impossible.

The steel gates were opened then and we were shouted at and screamed at to move inside. We had to walk a gauntlet down the tracks, between two lines of SS, their guard dogs snarling and growling at us. We immediately found ourselves in a large open area and the first thing I noticed was that there were few SS once we were inside. That could only mean one thing — the security was so tight that they didn't need to waste manpower on us once we were there.

We were marched past a huge building with a chimney that billowed smoke and gave out a sickly sweet stench. I wondered if the kitchen was situated there, and hoped that at least it meant we'd eat now, although the smell was really vile. There was a grapevine of news that started up right away, and before long I heard that we were in a place called Buchenwald. Then as we were walking, a guard came up beside me and said, "The only way out of here is through that chimney." When he saw the look on my face he laughed. I thought I might be sick, even though I had no food in my stomach to throw up. Was that smell *human flesh?* What kind of nightmare was this?

We were taken to a large grey building and split into groups of about fifty. I was in the second group. We were herded into a big room and told to strip. I had just gotten my clothes back! We were pushed into a line and I heard groans and moans coming from the front — I wondered if this was the beginning of an interrogation or even torture. As I got to the front, though, I saw a barber who was shaving heads. From the cries coming from big strong men, I figured this was not going to be any fun at all.

When it was my turn the "barber" didn't so much shave my head as tear the hair out from the roots. I too cried out despite my determination not to.

From there we went straight into a shower room. Although the water was freezing cold and hurt my head where I was raw from the shave, still, it was the first time I'd had any water on me since the doctor's house and it felt wonderful, even with no soap. I made sure to scrub my feet because I was worried that with the open wounds I might get an infection that could turn deadly very quickly.

Then I was shoved into another line, where I heard more cries and groans. When I reached the front I was confronted by a guard who was seated with a tub between his knees. He took a brush, dipped it in the tub and covered me with something orange, which burned as if ants were biting me. From the smell I figured it was some kind of disinfectant. I suddenly remembered jumping into a pile of leaves when I was about ten years old, not realizing it was filled with ants, and the agony that had caused. This was about a hundred times worse.

Then I was handed a shirt and pants and clogs. I noticed that I was one of the lucky ones, because only a few men were given shoes. I didn't turn them down though, because of the cuts on my feet. No one was given clothes that fit and since I was taller than most I looked around and found a fellow who was swimming in his. We switched both tops and bottoms, and I felt that at least I could manage.

A tin bowl was then shoved into my hands and I was told to get in line. I did. I noticed that our group was now much smaller. We were then taken to a desk where I gave my name, rank and service number.

"I demand to be recognized under the rules of the Geneva Convention."

The man behind the desk didn't even bother looking up.

He said, "You are a *Terrorflieger* and will be held in a *kleines Lager*. You will have no access to the Red Cross and no recognition as a prisoner of war." Then he waved me away.

Despite the terrors of the train ride, I had held on to the hope that we were on our way to a POW camp. Now we appeared to be in one of the dreaded concentration camps we'd heard so many horrible rumours about and perhaps no one even knew we were here! If the Red Cross didn't know about us, there would be no parcels.

126

If the Luftwaffe didn't know, we'd never be treated as POWs. We could die in this camp and there would be no help for us. I thought about the German POWs at home who were being treated honourably, with three hot meals a day and books to read and clean clothes and water and soap and clean bathrooms! And this was how we were to be treated!

The worst was the feeling of total and complete helplessness.

I followed the others out of the building and could see that it might be the downed air crews who were being herded together. We were taken past more and more long, low grey buildings and through two more gates until the guards stopped us in an open area surrounded by barbed wire and left us there. Lester, Trent and James joined me and they had picked up some news.

Trent spoke German well. He pointed to some men who were in the middle of an argument and told me that one of them was called a *Kapo*, a prisoner who acted as a guard for the Nazis, and that the other two men were high-ranking Allied officers. "I hear that one," he said, pointing, "is a squadron leader from New Zealand, and that one," he pointed to the other fellow, "is a colonel from the States."

What a relief! I couldn't believe our luck to have high-ranking officers here who were used to command and who could take charge, and who could hopefully lead us through and then out of this mess we were in.

It seemed that our new leaders weren't winning *this* argument, though. Word soon spread that we had missed the evening meal, that there were no barracks for us, and we were to sleep outside. We were apparently being held in a quarantine camp before being placed in a hut. The area we were in was called "Little Camp" in English — I suppose that's what *kleines Lager* meant. There were five big tents, but we weren't allowed into those, so I guessed they must be full. It looked like we had one option and that was to drop right where we were onto the rocky ground. There were already what looked like thousands gathered on the ground all around us, with more arriving every minute. Soon the Resistance fighters who'd been on the train with us were marched in. They huddled together beside us.

Blankets were given out but there was only one for about every three men. I lay down but there was no way to get comfortable. The ground was made up of hard, lumpy rock and stones. It was a warm night at least. I hoped we wouldn't still be here in a month when the fall weather would make it impossible to be outside.

I tried not to think too far ahead. Just get through tonight, I told myself. One thing at a time. Pretend you're camping at Winnipeg Beach. In the morning you'll get up and go for a swim in the lake and in the afternoon you'll eat hot dogs and french fries. And somehow I drifted off.

Chapter Twenty-One
August 21, 1944

When I woke up it was still dark and I expected to
see a tent over my head and to have Jenny kicking
at me through her sleeping bag, the way she always
did. Was it possible to awake from a dream into a
nightmare? Because instead of Jenny I looked up
to see James shaking me to get up, saying we had
to go to something called an *Appell* or roll call.
I followed the others to a large square where we,
along with the rest of the camp, had to line up and
be counted. It was just becoming light. The *Kapos*
counted us once, but apparently the numbers
didn't fit so they counted us again. The sun came
up and began to beat down on our heads. At first I
was thankful for the heat, because the damp from
sleeping on the rocks had seeped into my bones.
But by the time they had counted us three more
times I began to feel dizzy. And there were thousands of emaciated prisoners to be counted.

After about the third count, a prisoner was
pushed onto a block of wood, which was set up in

front of the rest of us. His shirt was taken off, and he was whipped! Whipped! I couldn't believe it. Each time I thought I'd seen the worst, I'd witness something else that I just couldn't credit. And then we were counted again and once more again. If anyone fell out of line they were kicked hard.

Finally we were allowed to leave and were herded back to our enclosure. Once there the squadron leader called us to order.

"Attention!"

I stood to attention, as did the rest of the men who'd been milling about hoping for some food.

The squadron leader then went on to make an impassioned speech, telling us that we were in a fine fix and that the "goons" — a term that seemed to fit the Germans perfectly, I thought — had completely violated the Geneva Convention and were determined to treat us like common thieves and criminals. He told us that we would conduct ourselves as befitted our training and as representatives of our countries. He ordered us to march to all roll calls as a unit. Then he directed us to get organized by reporting to a commanding officer for each country and to give our names and details to that officer.

Quickly I gathered with the other Canadians and was very happy to recognize some faces I hadn't seen yet. As I gave my home address in Winnipeg and my other particulars, my spirits started to improve. At least we would be under military command now and would work together for the best outcome for all of us. It seemed we were twenty-six Canadians in a group of one hundred and sixty-eight Allied airmen.

It was shortly afterward that "lunch" appeared. Not quite the hot dogs and french fries I'd been dreaming of the night before. We put our bowls out and the *Kapos* slopped some liquid into them. I looked at it and gagged. Worms were swimming all over the top. James actually laughed out loud.

"Well, well," he said, "at least they've given us some protein. Must be a mistake. Don't let them see or they'll take it away!"

I had to smile, despite myself.

"Drink up," he said. "Beggars can't be choosers."

I remembered eating a worm when I was a kid, as a dare. This couldn't be worse, could it?

I drank it down. I gagged once or twice but managed not to throw it back up again. Then I was given a piece of bread — more sawdust than bread, it turned out. But I choked that down too, although later on my stomach didn't thank me.

"Have you heard?" James said.

"What?"

"The goons" — that term seemed to be catching on quickly — "have ordered us all to work in the factories here. Apparently they're making parts for the German planes and guns and such."

"I imagine we say yes or we die," I said. "I think I might rather die. I couldn't in good conscience help the Nazis in their war effort."

"Easy to say," said Les, "until you're standing in front of a firing squad."

"I want to see what's really happening in that place with the chimneys. I heard someone call it the crematorium," I said. "Anyone else?"

"Why?" Trent asked.

"A guard told me that was the smell of human flesh. He said the only way out of here was up those chimneys," I answered. "But I can't believe it. I want to know what kind of a place this is. My dad always said, 'Knowledge is power, ignorance is never bliss.'"

"I'm up for a little trip," James said.

"Me too," agreed Trent.

Les said he was going to help finish up the lists that needed to be made.

The three of us started out. It was quite easy to get back to the building we wanted to find out about.

There was a small brick building attached to the larger building with the chimney. We looked through a window. That's when I saw at least fifty naked bodies piled one on top of each other.

I turned away, retching.

"We're in hell," I muttered aloud. "This must be hell."

A man who looked exactly like a walking skeleton hobbled up and stood in front of us. He had a green triangle attached to his pyjama top over a yellow triangle, so together it made a six-pointed star. He spoke German, but Trent translated for us.

"New here?" he asked.

"We're Canadian airmen," I answered. "We shouldn't be here!"

"None of us should be here," he replied.

"What is that? What happened to them?" I asked, pointing to the dead bodies.

He shrugged. "Murder, starvation, beaten to death, worked to death in the factories where we're forced to help the German war machine. Maybe one of the experiments in the medical block — injected with experimental vaccine, or killed for their tattoos. The commandant's wife likes to use decorated skins to make lampshades and book covers."

Was he joking with me? Some sort of horrible sick joke? Maybe he'd been driven mad.

I wondered if the star on his shirt meant something. I'd noticed all prisoners at the roll call wore different triangles. "What does that mean?" I asked him, pointing to his star.

"Jewish," he said, "and the other one — green — criminal."

Were we talking to a murderer? I guess he read my mind because he almost smiled. He said, "All Jews are criminals or political or something else — and that way, with one triangle on top of the other . . . well, it's ironic, but we end up with a Jewish star." He paused. "I come every day to see if I recognize any bodies. It's the only way to find out who's been killed or who's died. You'll do the same pretty soon."

He pointed over to another building. "That's where they do the experiments. They shrink heads. But I wouldn't advise going over there to look. You can come here, no problem, but that's a place I'd stay away from."

I wanted to ask him something but didn't know how. Finally I said, "A good friend of mine is Jewish and he told me that Jews were being rounded up. He told me there was torture, even murder."

"But you didn't believe it?"

"I don't know what to believe, now, after seeing that," I said, jerking my head toward the bodies.

"We didn't believe it either," the man said sadly. "My name is Leo. I'm from Frankfurt. All the Jews were rounded up there and shipped east. In Poland they were either killed on the spot or sent to extermination camps."

"Extermination camps?" I said.

"Camps built just to kill Jews. I've heard they use gas because they can kill faster that way than by shooting them." He paused. "It's my birthday today. I'm twenty-two years old."

"But . . . you're close to *my* age?" That didn't seem possible to me.

"I look ninety, I'm sure," he said. "We're slave labour here — Jews, Poles, Russians, Czechs — and when we're done and can't work and fall down on the way to the rock quarry, or slump over in the factory, then they shoot us or hang us because we're no more use to them. I think I might last another week."

All the time Trent had been translating, and when he said that his voice dropped and it looked like he could hardly get the words out.

"Is there anything we can do for you?" James asked.

"Yes," he replied, "if you would."

"What?" James said.

"Remember me."

"What is your full name?" asked James.

"Leo Cohen." And then he shook each of our hands and added, "Maybe there will be no Jews left in Europe when the war is over. Before we are liberated we will all be killed. So it would be nice to be remembered."

And with that he drifted away and we walked back to our part of the camp.

"Maybe ignorance *is* bliss," James said.

Trent looked shaken. "I'd rather not have seen that."

"Or heard what he had to say," added James.

"But there are millions of Jews in Europe, aren't there?" I asked. "How could they kill them all? It's not possible! And why? Why?"

No one answered me. And I couldn't understand it. I couldn't understand anything at all, it seemed.

Chapter Twenty-Two
August 24, 1944

It was our fourth day in Buchenwald and certain things had been established. We were under strict orders by our commanders to always behave in a way that would bring credit to our uniforms — even if we weren't wearing them. We were to stay together in this area, only leaving to fetch food rations or visit the latrines (that word didn't describe the horror and filth of what we were forced to use). We were to avoid the SS, could meet with other prisoners, but only if we didn't talk politics, and no one was to attempt an escape for the moment. In the meantime, every day at noon the two commanders would march off in military form and try to get a meeting with the Camp Commandant, to insist we be recognized as POWs. But so far, no luck. Every day they came back with nothing to report.

Still, the grapevine at the camp was better than a telephone system and soon it was well known that our group of flyers had arrived. We began to get visits from other prisoners. We quickly learned what all the different triangles meant that were stitched to men's tops, such as red for political prisoners, pink for homosexuals, purple for Jehovah's Witnesses. Alongside the triangle was the letter signifying their country, *F* for France and so on. It seemed that there were prisoners from all over the world. We also learned what and who the *Kapos* were. Just regular prisoners, but given special privileges — more food, parcels from home, a separate room — as rewards for taking control over the other men. It was these *Kapos* who advised our leaders to keep a low profile and not make too big a fuss. They promised that they would try to find us indoor accommodations as soon as something opened up.

Our commanders were absolutely firm on one point. We would not work in the factories, no matter what. We were not slave labour, but prisoners of war, period.

My spirits were pretty darn low. I had barely slept, was always hungry and yet my gut was a mess. The frequent trips to the *Abort* — the latrine — were the stuff of horror. I was itchy and filthy, and finding it harder and harder to believe in the good world out there with people in it like Mom and Pops and Jenny.

I stared up at the clear blue sky and imagined that it was the same blue sky over Winnipeg and that I was out walking by the Red River, looking into its muddy waters, dreaming about nothing in particular. That's what I missed so much. The days when there was nothing much to worry about, days when I thought I was bored. What I'd give to be bored like that again!

I heard the sirens before I could see anything. I hoped this wasn't a false alarm and that I'd actually get to see some kites in the air — some of our boys! More sirens went off and the din was amazing. And then I saw them.

It had to be the Yanks! They were fearless. They always flew the daylight missions. Probably Forts. I judged the bombers to be about 30 miles away. I also counted hundreds! And knowing my directions well, plus remembering the route we took to reach Buchenwald, I figured they were heading for Weimar and the rail yards. It was beautiful, and yet we could hear no noise at all from them. I saw orange and yellow bursts of flame and black puffs of smoke. Then ack-ack fire and two planes went down right away.

I found myself glued to the spot, thrilled that we were not alone, that almost above us were flyers ready to destroy the Germans! And that's when I saw about sixty or so planes break away from the formation and head straight for us! I looked around, ready to run, and quickly realized that there was absolutely nowhere *to* run! But I didn't care! I yelled at the top of my lungs, "Come on, fellows! Do your best! Wipe this place to the ground!"

"Hold on there," James said, coming up beside me. "I'd rather not be bombed to smithereens by a bunch of cowboys." At that he pulled me down to the ground. There was no cover for us, not even the flimsy barracks, so we just lay there and waited. It wasn't long before we saw the smoke flare from the lead plane that told the others where to drop their load. We heard the sound of the bombs, a whistle, a screech, then a rumble like a train and then the earth shook and then shook again and shook again.

I risked a look up to see another large group of planes break off and head our way. And suddenly I worried that I'd left my name in those markings on the wall of Fresnes prison. What if someone saw that and had contacted my parents? What if they now hoped I was alive and then never knew I'd died here. After all, no one knew we were here, outside of the goons in charge. Like Michel on the train, I'd be missing in action forever.

And yet, despite all that, I didn't care! After what I'd seen in the last few days I was happy they were going after the camp. And it was a good target for sure. Those factories were using slave labour to pump out guns and armaments and airplane parts. And those poor prisoners wouldn't have to work in the plants if there were no plants to work in.

That's when the second wave hit, first the white puff of smoke and then the thud, whistle, screech and rumble of a train. The ground shook more and more until black smoke started to rise up and the air seemed to heat up as if we were in some kind of hot-air bath. I could feel stuff hitting me, nothing big enough to really hurt me, but there was debris flying everywhere. I wondered if this would be what it felt like to be in a hurricane or maybe in a tornado with things whipped all around you and the very earth beneath you shaking. And of course at any second something very big could land on you or crush you and that would be that. But slowly the sound of the bombs faded and another sound took its place — the whooshing sound of a wind that had probably risen from the heat of the blast and from fire, which now seemed to be everywhere. From the way things had gone up in flames, I could tell that the Yanks had dropped incendiaries.

I sat up and looked around. I couldn't see the sky anymore, the air was so black, but I couldn't hear any more planes or the telltale *whoosh* of the bombs coming down either. It was most likely over. Quickly everyone checked, and outside of one fellow who'd caught a piece of shrapnel in the shoulder, we seemed all right.

"See," I said to James, "Now that was a fine piece of flying!"

Before we had a chance to celebrate that we'd made it through alive, guards rushed into our compound and shouted at us. "Follow. *Raus! Raus!*"

My heart sank. Were they going to make examples of us? It would make sense — if you thought the way the Nazis thought. We were flyers. Flyers had just destroyed a good part of the camp. We should die.

Chapter Twenty-Three
August 24, 1944

James, Trent, me and some other flyers I didn't know too well fell in and followed one of the guards — in formation, though, as we'd been ordered by our commanders. Others in our group were also being rushed out.

There was an inferno in the section of the camp where the factories had been. We were told that we were to help put out the fires, and that we'd been chosen because we were used to acting as a unit and could work together quickly. So someone *had* noticed that we were acting like POWs, not regular prisoners. And at least they weren't about to shoot us.

There was no water to be had, so one of our men suggested that we pull down the building next to the one on fire, to create a firewall. The guards seemed pleased with that idea and, using our hands, we pulled at the hot wood and literally broke apart the building next to the fire. I was one of the lucky ones because I had my clogs — most of the others had to work in their bare feet.

I wasn't sure we should even be helping at all, but decided that if our leaders were all right with it, so was I. And the guards seemed so frantic that I had no doubt we would have been shot if we'd said no. We must have worked for hours until the fire seemed ready to burn itself out. Word spread that most of the factories had been levelled, the SS barracks had been destroyed and the commandant's wife was dead. That was all good. Not as good was that when the factories were levelled, we knew that they'd been filled with workers and there must have been a huge loss of life.

"Come!" said a voice in front of me.

I looked up to see a guard pointing to the small group of us — five, including Trent and James — that had been working right near the edge of the fire, pulling down boards. My heart started beating hard again, wondering if *this* was it — were we going to be killed now? We followed him into a small hut and the guard motioned to a rough wood table — on it was a loaf of white bread and some jars of jam. He pointed to the benches and we sat down. Then he cut thick slices off the bread, passed them to us and invited us to spread them with preserves. I took as big a scoop as I could. It looked like apple and when I bit into it I realized it was. It was the best thing I'd tasted in months.

And then he poured hot coffee for us into mugs — real coffee, not the acorn water we were given every morning for breakfast.

Silently I thanked the Yanks again. A beautiful bombing run and to top it off, a real meal. What a day!

We slept outside again as usual that night, but for the first time since arriving I was able to get some rest despite the rocks sticking into me and the cold seeping into my bones. Except, when I fell asleep I dreamed. And I dreamed about Max. I dreamed that he was Leo Cohen and that Leo Cohen was Max and that they both ended up on that pile of corpses. But neither of them was really dead. And Max kept calling, "I'm not dead! I'm not dead! Sam! Get me out of here!" I woke up in a sweat despite the cold night air.

What if Max had been caught? What if they had discovered he was a Jew? What if he had been thrown in with the Jewish prisoners instead of being recognized as an Allied airman? Somehow I had to find out if he was in the camp. But how? There were tens of thousands of inmates. And we were now under strict orders not to wander around the camp, so how could I do reconnaissance? And to make my search even more difficult, because our few meagre possessions had started to disappear at night when we slept, the leaders decided that our area would be out of bounds for anyone outside of Air Force, so we mounted a guard each night. I didn't want to slip past our own men.

I sat up shivering the rest of the night and watched the sun peek over the horizon the next morning. Right after our morning cup of acorn coffee, the *Kapos* herded us into another compound. We marched in formation again and that reminded me that yes, I was RCAF!

A guard began to question us about what our non-military jobs were, because the camp needed men to help them rebuild. They wanted builders and electricians and anyone who could work. The squadron leader stepped forward and set the example, followed by the colonel. He gave his name, rank and service number and refused to offer any more information about himself and what he could do. When it was my turn, the guard stood over me, glaring. I stared back and calmly gave my name, rank and service number. I was not going to work for them no matter what!

An SS officer arrived then and started to yell and scream and threaten our leaders. They stood firm and stared ahead, perfectly calm. Eventually the Nazi spat in disgust and stalked off. And we marched back to our rocky, miserable home.

Chapter Twenty-Four
August 29, 1944

Ten days. Ten days out in the open when James came up to me with an actual smile on his face.

"We're getting into a hut," he said.

And that actually made me smile too.

By some miracle it hadn't rained the whole time we'd been outside, but today the clouds were gathering. I'd been staring at the sky all morning, transfixed, sure that our luck was about to run out and that in no time we'd all be soaked through. I was getting weak from lack of food and there were the sores on the bottom of my feet that just wouldn't heal. Others in our group had bad coughs, and some gruesome infections. I was lucky that so far I'd been spared the worst. My Viking constitution, James joked.

When we got inside I looked around. Row after row of bunks or shelves lined both sides of the hut. There was a large wash basin at the front, big enough for about six to wash at a time, three tables with benches, and in the middle of the barracks, or *Lager* as they called it, a wood stove. There was a notice board at the front door, stating that there were 757 prisoners, and we added 168. We soon learned that there were 400 boys aged eight to fourteen, and the rest were Poles.

At least, I thought, we were out of the elements. It wasn't long after we got inside that the rain began to pelt down.

Within an hour of being inside, a young boy struck up a conversation with me. Or tried — he spoke no English. Although I kept telling myself that nothing should surprise me, I wondered why on earth children were being held as prisoners.

He spoke German rapidly and pointed to his brown triangle. I called Trent over and he translated for us. It turned out that these boys were Romani — what we called Gypsies. They were treated the same as the Jews — not considered pure of race — and had been rounded up just as the Jews had. They had been working as slave labour but were afraid that any day they would be shipped off to be murdered. Thrown away like garbage. The boy had large brown eyes and would grow up to be a dashing young man. But now he wouldn't get that chance unless a miracle happened.

As we spoke I started to scratch. And scratch. The boy laughed. He pointed to my pants and motioned for me to take them off. I did. He showed me the little critters already hiding inside the seams. I was really revolted. Bedbugs! I guess there had been one good thing about being outside. He taught me how to go through the seams and crunch the little beggars between my fingernails.

"What's your name?" I asked, Trent translating for me.

"Luca," he answered.

"Where are your parents?" I asked.

"Don't know where my mother and sister are," he said. "Many were taken by train somewhere if they couldn't work. My papa worked for a few months, but he died."

Luca stayed with me and Trent for the rest of the day and the day after that, and showed us the ropes. He seemed to enjoy being the one in the know, the one who could tell us what was what. Those first days consisted mostly of trying to control the bedbugs and the lice. We threw out all the straw and bedding and washed everything down over and over and over again. Luca showed us his pants, the pockets turned out so that bugs couldn't live there, and we all quickly caught on until everyone was wearing their pants with the pockets inside out.

I was trying to teach Luca some English on

our third morning in the barracks when the SS stormed in and started screaming at the Romani boys.

"Raus! Raus!"

I stood in front of Luca, thinking that maybe I could push him under a bunk and then hide him with the other prisoners later — maybe the Russians would take him — but an SS guard shoved me aside, picked Luca up by the collar and threw him into the crowd of other boys. I watched them go and felt such despair and disgust, I wondered if it was even worth carrying on.

Chapter Twenty-Five
September 30, 1944

James came up to me as I was playing cards with Trent and some others, and said, "I have some news that might cheer you up. Some Danish policemen have just arrived. You should go see them."

"Cheer me up? I can't be happy that anyone has been captured and sent *here* of all places," I replied.

"I understand," he said. "And you know I didn't mean I was happy about it either. Still, go see them."

As I made my way over to the new group clustered together on the rocks, I couldn't help but realize just how long we'd already been stuck in this hellhole. Weeks, not days as we had hoped. And the brutality and horror of what we saw every day seemed to worsen as time went on, not lessen. Just that morning we had seen a *Kapo* beaten to death right in front of our hut.

I tried to put the image of that out of my mind as I approached some of the newcomers and spoke to a few of them. It *was* good to hear the language my grandfather had taught me when I was young. Also they didn't arrive like us — with nothing. They were wearing their own clothes, carrying suitcases, just like normal people! They even had Red Cross packages under their arms. There must have been a thousand of them. I was able to speak to a few fellows in Danish, but soon found it was unnecessary, as many of them spoke excellent English.

A fellow called Lars told me how they had been captured.

"There was an air raid," he said, "so of course we all responded. When we were at our posts the SS popped up out of nowhere, and we were arrested."

"The French *gendarmes* weren't ever arrested," I said. "So why were you?"

Lars chuckled. "I suppose we weren't as good at carrying out the Germans' orders," he answered. "We would forget to arrest people. We were very slow carrying out their orders. When they held their rallies no one would show up, including the police. Finally they said we were part of the Resistance. Some were, I'm sure, but most of us just tried to do our best for our people."

"So no one came to the rallies the Nazis held?" I asked.

"Maybe a few Nazi sympathizers. That's it. I suppose the Nazis were a little angry about the strikes, too," he added.

"Strikes?"

"Yes, and how we scuttled our navy so they couldn't use it and how we managed to get so many of our Jewish neighbours out of the country and safely to Sweden." He paused then added, "Anyway, we just did what anyone would have done under the same circumstances."

But was that true? From my own experience and my own betrayal, it seemed that some of the French had not behaved that way at all.

I wandered back to my group. Trent asked me if I had heard anything about Max, as everyone knew I was always on the lookout for him. I said I hadn't and Trent assured me that was a good thing. I hoped so. I was beginning to believe that Max, at least, had escaped.

Just after our so-called dinner we were told by our leaders that we were going to the movies! We marched into a real theatre that had about five hundred seats. Once I had sat down between Trent and James, for one brief moment it felt like everything was normal and we were on leave together at the movies. In a way, that made the nightmare quality of being in the camp even worse though.

We were then forced to sit through a newsreel about how well the enemy was doing, with lots of bloody shots of our troops being slaughtered. It was sickening. There was a movie after the newsreel, all in German of course, but Trent kept up a running commentary, making up silly things that the actors never would have said and keeping me and James in stitches. When the two leads kissed passionately, Trent had the actress say, "My, you have bad breath." And in return, the actor said, "That's nothing compared to your B.O." And Trent hardly stopped for breath, managing to write an entire movie script in the moment.

That night I slept — after meeting the Danes and going to the movies, I felt more human than I had in ages.

Chapter Twenty-Six
October 19, 1944

It was too crowded to be in the hut so we stayed
outside on the rocks during the day. We'd sleep
inside at night, squashed together on the shelves.
We had so little space that if one person had to
turn over, everyone had to turn over. It would
have been funny if it hadn't been so uncomfort-
able. But it's all what you are used to — compared
to the hard rocks outside, it was far better.

The days grew monotonous, the routine only
interrupted by bursts of brutality we were forced
to witness. Sometimes we'd play cards, created
from pieces of scrap paper someone had gathered and marked up well enough to do the trick.
Sometimes we'd relive old hockey games, argu-
ing about our teams and who would win the next
cup.

Alex, a Russian who had made friends with us
shortly after we'd arrived, came up to me while I
was sitting on the rock pile, my face turned into
the sun. He had been one of the prisoners who had

helped us get more blankets, extra food and shoes when we flyers first arrived.

He sat down wearily and said, matter of factly, "Five hundred a day — that's how many of us Russians they are killing. Over the other end of the camp — just outside at the west? Used to be a horse stable there. Now they use it as a killing factory. The crematorium is going full steam ahead again — all fixed up after the Allies' raid." He shook his head sadly. "October twenty-fourth. That's your time." He patted my shoulder. "Sorry. But better you know."

I knew he meant that was the day we were to be executed. I also knew that today was the nineteenth. So, less than a week left?

I thought back to a week ago. One morning we had been woken by "Ten hut!" and saw it was the American colonel.

Of course we were all squashed together on the bunks, so getting up and scrambling into formation was quite a feat, but we finally managed. Our leaders instructed us to speak to some officers that had appeared out of nowhere — officers we realized were from the Luftwaffe. I was afraid I was going to be asked about the Resistance and I vowed that I wouldn't give up any information even at this late date, when hopefully no one in France would be in danger. But when it was my turn I was just asked my name, rank and service number and where I'd been captured. I looked at the Luftwaffe officers and a small hope started to grow — perhaps we would make it out alive. Now I wondered if that hope was to be dashed completely.

I wanted to find Lars and ask him if he had heard anything, but first I had to go to the infirmary and visit Les. The open wound in his arm had become so infected that you could see the bone.

I sat on his cot and asked him how he was doing.

"Every day an SS goon walks through checking the patients," he said to me. "If you look too weak and he points at you, you'll get a needle and be dead in a couple hours. The doctor has been moving me from bed to bed so the goon doesn't realize I've been here so long."

I didn't know what to say so I waited for him to go on.

"Yesterday I saw them wrap a guy in a wet rubber blanket and in a few hours his pneumonia got worse and he suffocated to death."

I thought to myself that only a few months ago, if someone had told me that one man would do that to another, I would have laughed at him. Now I knew better. Now I didn't doubt for a moment that what Les was telling me was the truth.

"But there's hope," I said. "The Luftwaffe has been here. Someone at least knows about us now. Don't give up."

"Canadians don't give up," he said, but his words said one thing, his eyes another.

I certainly wasn't going to tell him what Alex had just told me. I hurried over to the Danes and searched out Lars.

"Ah, my friend!" he said when he spotted me heading toward him. "Just the person I wanted to see. Look, I have some clean cloths here and some antiseptic! Let me have a look at your feet. Plus we all just got more packages from the Red Cross and I want you to take some."

I'd been hobbling around for days. The sores that I got when James and I had to dig Michel's grave had never healed, and no wonder — we were living in pure filth.

Lars had managed to scrounge some clean water and he bathed my wounds, cleaned them up and wrapped them in clean cloths. It reminded me of my mother and how she would take care of me when I was little and how much sweetness and goodness there was in the world — even here in this hell. Then he gave me a clean pair of pants and a clean shirt.

"You want to be a doctor, correct?" he asked me.

I nodded.

"Have you heard this one? A waiter walks over to Dr. Jensen's table. He says, 'I have sautéed liver, frog's legs and boiled tongue.'

"The doctor answers, 'I'm here to eat, not to listen to your problems!'"

It was so silly I had to laugh. How could Lars keep his sense of humour in the midst of all this?

I asked him something else though. "How is it that you're receiving Red Cross packages and food and clothes, and no one else has such luck?"

"Luck?" he said. "I don't think it is luck, my friend. From the moment we were arrested, the Danish Red Cross has kept track of us, insisted on visits, insisted on knowing where we were. They are a real thorn in the Germans' side!"

"The hardest thing for most of us," I said, "is that no one knows where we are, that our parents have no idea what's happened to us and might never know. Every day our commanders try to get a message to the Luftwaffe, and it seemed as if maybe we'd made progress because some of them actually came to see us." I paused, barely able to get the words out. "But now I hear we're to be executed."

"I've heard that too," Lars said quietly. "But where there's life, there's hope. And without hope we have nothing. So don't give up."

When I didn't answer he said, "Besides, Danes don't give up. We're very stubborn!"

I felt so downhearted that for a few moments I didn't speak. I guess I'd been hoping he'd tell me that he'd heard we were going to be saved and sent to a POW camp! When I did speak it was difficult to express to him what I'd been dwelling on lately.

"There's something I've been worried about," I said.

"Go on."

I wasn't sure exactly how to say it or even what I meant, so I struggled to put this feeling into words. "I was brought up to always see the best in people. And I worry . . . well, I worry that maybe if I'd been a German, I would have supported Hitler because he promised to make everyone's life better, and maybe I would have trusted him. I mean, could I have ended up being a Nazi? Or supporting them like so many Germans did?"

Lars thought about what I had said before he replied.

"I think that there is one very simple way to discover whether someone deserves your trust or not — like a leader or someone in power, or even a friend. 'Do unto others as you would have others do unto you.' Would you want to be treated the way Hitler treated his political rivals? Rounded up? Sent away? Beaten. Murdered. Would you want to be treated the way he treated the Jewish people? And I don't think that you would have followed him. Because seeing the best in people doesn't mean you go blind!"

"No, I guess it doesn't."

And to make me feel better he gave me some cheese. Real cheese! Along with chocolate and biscuits. And despite the terror, eating some real food did actually make me feel better.

Chapter Twenty-Seven
October 20, 1944

Somehow I had managed to drop into a deep sleep, so it was a shock to be abruptly woken up by SS troopers storming into our hut and ordering us to follow them. What was going to happen? Was the Russian right? Were we going straight to the execution hut outside the gates?

The first thing I noticed was that Les and about a dozen others weren't there, maybe too sick to go, so there were only about a hundred and fifty of us moving out. At that point I didn't know whether Les and the others were the lucky ones or we were. We formed up as a unit and, as we did every day going to the roll call, marched in military formation to a building used as a storehouse. I was handed the clothes I wore when I'd arrived here — they had actually been cleaned and disinfected, so they weren't too bad. And anyway, why give them to me if they were just going to shoot me? On the other hand, anything was possible with the SS, so I still wasn't sure that we were safe.

We then marched to roll call. There we were separated from the others and counted over and over again. It was raining and I was soaked through but I barely felt it. All I could feel was my heart beating. It was so loud I thought the entire camp could hear it. Was it possible that our leaders had pulled off a miracle and had us declared POWs? Or was it another Nazi ploy and the goons were hoping that was what we'd think and then we'd go quietly to our deaths? Oh yes. I think I knew them well by now, how they thought. They wouldn't want to bother fighting us, or troubling with a group who might still put up a show if we discovered that we were to be slaughtered. No, they would lie to us. They would tell us we were going to a POW camp. And when we were pacified they would mow us down the way they did Michel.

Rumours swirled from one man to the next — some said we were going to a POW camp near the Austrian border. Others said we were being sent to another concentration camp. Still others said we were going straight to a firing squad.

An hour went by. Then another hour, then another hour, then another hour and on and on until we'd been standing in the rain for six hours. I remembered that one day we'd stood for five hours in the sun and some of the men had fainted and we'd had to hold them up and pretend they were fine so they weren't taken away. No one fainted today but that was because we refused. We refused to give in!

Sometime in the afternoon SS troops appeared. They had machine guns and dogs and grenades. And then the huge gate opened. Opened. This was it.

We marched out the main gate and were herded to a railway siding. We were yelled at to stop once we reached a train and the train's boxcars.

And that's when something happened that was totally unexpected. The SS guards just marched off, and in their place, men in the blue uniforms of the Luftwaffe took their place!

For the first time I felt that maybe, just maybe, we were not going to be shot.

The doors to the cattle cars were pulled open. About thirty of us were told to get in. We did. And so did two guards. By this time I was shaking so hard from excitement, fear and cold that I thought my teeth would rattle out. The cattle car was freezing and we huddled together for warmth. Finally the train jerked and began to move. Could this be true? Were we really leaving this nightmare behind?

The conditions on the cattle car were the exact ones as before, but at least there was plenty of room. James and Trent were on board with me and after a while going over and over what might be happening to us, we got bored and looked for something to occupy our minds and keep ourselves from going crazy wondering about the possibilities.

I was talking hockey to James when the rest of the men got involved and we decided to make hockey teams. We were too weak to actually get up and move about, so we talked ourselves through an entire game. There might have been an unrealistic number of, "He shoots, he scores!" shouted out, but our guards left us alone and at that point we were happy for small miracles.

Chapter Twenty-Eight
October 22, 1944

It was around noon when the train screeched to a halt. We'd been travelling for two and a half days. I looked out the opening and saw the word *Sagan* but couldn't remember having seen it on any of my maps. I wasn't sure if we were still in Germany or if we were now in Poland. The guards were packing up their gear and we were told to get off the train.

We jumped out, formed up and then began a march down a small path beside the train. I looked around. There was a pine forest on one side, the train on the other. The sun was shining, but it was cool. I had just a shirt and pants on, and since I had no fat left at all, or muscle either for that matter, it was only minutes before I started to shiver. Also I still wasn't quite convinced we were going to a camp. At that I almost laughed out loud. What other Allied airmen would be so happy to get to a POW camp?

It must have been about a half-mile when we turned a corner and there it was, the camp! It was a series of long low buildings behind barbed-wire fencing. There were watchtowers all around with guards whose rifles were pointed right at us. There was an outer platform with machine guns affixed to it and searchlights as well. At one time I might have found the sight intimidating, frightening even. Now there was almost something comforting in it because it was the way I expected a POW camp to look.

The guards counted us at least three times before finally opening the gate and letting us in. We heard right away that we were, in fact, in Stalag Luft III. We were told by an officer that we would be admitted and then sent into a building where we would get rid of our clothes and be taken to the showers.

A shower! Heaven! The water wasn't hot but it was warm, and there was a sliver of soap. I scrubbed and scrubbed until I felt like I must be shining. I couldn't help but notice all the open sores I had all over my body, things I'd tried to ignore while in Buchenwald.

I was then issued military kit, but it was a mix of Army and Air Force. I didn't care. It was clean. I was given my own boots back! Imagine — they had kept track of them from our arrival at Buchenwald. Now *that* was organization. And a coat. A warm winter coat! And a new towel and a new toothbrush!

We were split up then and assigned to quarters,

depending on what was available. James and I were sent with eight others to a central barracks. As we walked I saw men playing football! That they had the energy for it said everything to me. And sure enough, the other inmates we saw looked almost healthy and well fed, at least compared to the prisoners of Buchenwald. They were smoking! They had full heads of hair! Some even had moustaches! Still, if you compared them to the way we all were before being captured, then you could see how they too had suffered at the hands of the goons.

We still had more paperwork to do — the goons took our pictures and wrote down our details. Then a fellow called Larry took us for a tour — there was even a music room. We were now separated from the Americans, which I thought was a shame as I'd grown quite close to them all during our two months in Buchenwald.

We were split up again. James and I said we'd meet up later and Larry took me to my living quarters. When I walked in I felt like I'd landed in heaven. I saw books, playing cards — real ones — a chess board, pipes, wash basins, water and soap. Someone had just made tea and offered me a cup. Real tea? As I drank, I was peppered with questions about where we'd come from. But when I answered them I was met with looks that said what I was telling them was hardly to be believed. And yet, it's not that they thought I was a liar, I don't think — maybe they just didn't want to believe it. I assured them that I hadn't wanted to believe it either, but that they should check with the others, especially our squadron leader, and they would see that it was true.

There was one thing and one thing alone that I wanted to do, and that was to write a letter home. I asked one of the fellows and he gave me a form and a pencil. The form was only 6 inches wide and 10 inches long. It had twenty-four ruled lines. There was so much to say. But in reality I knew the censors would read it and that I couldn't write anything about France because I wouldn't want to give anything away. I couldn't write anything about Buchenwald because they would just censor it. I couldn't even write anything about my ops. I sat there and thought about what I wished I could say, and some of it surprised even me.

Thinking back over the last few months, I realized that everything I thought I had known was wrong. I wondered how these Nazis — thugs, really — were able to not only take over in Germany, but almost take over the world. Was it because we couldn't imagine the evil they represented? I thought that might be it. I simply hadn't believed that the actions and deeds of the Germans were possible. Even after witnessing it myself I found it hard to believe! The world could not imagine such evil. And because we denied it, we weren't ready . . . and before we knew it — well, it was almost too late.

Someone gave me a second cup of tea. I began to write:

October 22, 1944

Dear Mother, Pops and Jenny:
I am in a POW camp. It's been a hard time. There is one thing I know for certain — this was all worth it. All I want now, though, is to come home. I dream of frikadeller *and* wienerbroed *and hot dogs and french fries and swimming at the beach and tobogganing in the winter and going to school.*
I just want to come home.

With love,
Sam

Epilogue

Sam's parents had remained hopeful that he was still alive because they'd received a letter from Max, who had managed to evade the Germans and had eventually reached the Allied lines. That had kept their hopes alive until Sam himself was able to write them. He endured many more hardships, including a forced march from Stalag Luft III in January 1945, in which some of the POWs died. Sam had other close calls before he made it safely back to England — just two days before Victory in Europe (VE) Day, May 8, 1945. On that day, while all around him people celebrated, Sam could think only of those who had perished.

When Sam finally returned home to his family — who were delirious with joy — they believed his story, of course, but so many others didn't that he soon stopped telling people he had been in a concentration camp.

It was hard for Sam that people didn't believe him. But he had other things on his mind. He wanted to go to university and study medicine. And he wanted to go out with Sadie Kobrinsky, so he asked her and she said yes right away. The two were never parted again. When their first son was born they named him Leo after Leo Cohen, the young man Sam had met in Buchenwald, so that Leo would be remembered, just as Sam had promised.

Although Max returned to Montreal after the war, he and Sam remained fast friends for the rest of their lives.

Historical Note

Canada's Contribution to the Air War

Canada entered the Second World War on September 10, 1939, one week after Britain and a full two years before the United States. During the First World War, many flyers had been recruited and trained in Canada for Britain. Similarly, when the Second World War broke out, Canada became a training ground for all Commonwealth flyers, under the British Commonwealth Air Training Plan (BCATP).

Canada played a major role in the training of aircrew for the Royal Air Force (RAF), the Royal Australian Air Force, and the Royal New Zealand Air Force, as well as for its own Royal Canadian Air Force (RCAF). It had the open spaces that enabled it to train pilots and other aircrew far away from the range of German aircraft, something Britain lacked.

The Royal Canadian Air Force ran the training program, in conjunction with the Canadian Flying Clubs Association, aviation companies and the Department of Transport. Though there were limited aircraft, trainers and airfields, training began on April 29, 1940. Aircrew candidates were transferred to Canada for training. Eventually, over one hundred and thirty-one thousand pilots, navigators, bomb aimers, wireless (radio) operators, air gunners and flight engineers graduated from the BCATP. Almost seventy-three thousand of these were Canadians.

BCATP graduates went where they were most needed for the war effort, with the RAF having the key say in this. Most squadrons had a mix of Commonwealth air forces represented, both aircrew and especially ground crew. No. 6 RCAF Bomber Group, established in January 1943, was still part of RAF Bomber Command.

Statistics from the Bomber Command Museum of Canada website indicate just how dangerous it was to be part of an aircrew fighting for the Allies. Only German U-boat forces and Allied Merchant Navy sailors had a lower chance of surviving the war than RAF Bomber Command aircrew:

- For every 100 men who joined, 45 were killed, 6 were wounded and 8 became prisoners of war.
- 120,000 airmen served; over 55,000 died.

- Over 10,000 Canadians were killed.
- A pilot's average lifespan was 6 weeks. Pilots who started flying at the start of the war had only a 10 percent chance of surviving.
- Between March of 1943 and February 1944 there was only a 16 percent survival rate for the crews of Halifax bombers.

Sir Arthur Harris of the RAF, the person who sent the men to battle, said this: "There are no words with which I can do justice to the aircrew who fought under my command. There is no parallel in warfare to such courage and determination in the face of danger over so prolonged a period."

He described them as having "a clear and highly conscious courage, by which the risk was taken with calm forethought. . . . It was, furthermore, the courage of the small hours, of men virtually alone, for at his battle station the airman is virtually alone. It was the courage of men with long-drawn apprehensions of daily 'going over the top.' Such devotion must never be forgotten!"

The French Resistance

The French Resistance is a term that encompasses all the anti-German movements in France during the Second World War. There were as many as nine major Resistance networks by the time Sam and his crew were shot down in the summer of 1944.

Resistance to the German forces began with individuals rejecting their own government's collaboration with the Germans who occupied France after the invasion on May 10, 1940. The prime minister of France, Marshal Pétain, negotiated France's surrender to Germany and authorized the French delegation to sign an armistice on June 22, 1940. Part of the agreement allowed an "independent" French government headquartered in Vichy, which came to be known as Vichy France (versus Occupied France in the north, which included Paris). The government of Vichy, with Pétain as Chief of State, collaborated with the Germans.

At first Resistance fighters did what they could with the few resources they had — they cut telephone lines, derailed trains or sent them to the wrong locations, killed or kidnapped German officers or soldiers when they could, and published underground newspapers. But soon many of these individuals joined together and formed all sorts of different groups, from the Communists to Jewish groups to the Maquis. The latter were fighters who hid in the forests and around the countryside, especially in the mountainous regions of France. Many had originally been conscripted to work in German factories and were to be sent away to Germany or further east to Poland, but instead joined a Resistance group.

By 1943 some of these Resistance groups had joined together under the leadership of Charles de Gaulle, a French officer who had fled to London and had begun working with the British government. The Resistance managed to send vital intelligence to the Allies about German troop movements. It went on the attack whenever possible, and it was the main reason so many Allied airmen survived after their planes were shot down.

The Resistance set up a number of escape routes to help return Allied flyers to Britain so that they could carry on the fight. An estimated three thousand American flyers and twenty-five hundred British flyers were sent to freedom along these escape routes. According to Don Lawson's *The French Resistance,* for every man who escaped, a Resistance operator lost his or her life.

Secrecy was of the utmost importance in the Resistance. Members of the small groups — cells

— often used false names so that any member who was captured could not give away the identities of the others under torture.

German reprisals for the Resistance's guerilla tactics were harsh. Successful raids against German targets sometimes meant that local civilians would be punished or killed by the German forces, to instill fear in the population and undercut local support for the Resistance.

After the Allied landing of June 6, 1944, in Normandy, the Resistance played a large role in the war effort, moving from sabotage, guerilla actions and maintaining escape routes to actual fighting alongside the Allied forces and supporting their advance against the Germans. But there were also French men and women who worked diligently for Pétain's Vichy government, especially after 1942 when the entire country was occupied by German forces. These "Vichyites" would infiltrate the Resistance, sabotage their efforts, and betray them to the German authorities.

The men and women of the Resistance endured hardship, possessed great courage, and made a great impact with often-limited resources. American General Dwight D. Eisenhower said that the Resistance had been "of inestimable value in the campaign."

The Holocaust

The United States Holocaust Memorial Museum defines the Holocaust as the "systematic, bureaucratic, state-sponsored persecution and murder of approximately six million Jews by the Nazi regime and its collaborators."

Adolf Hitler was voted into office by the German people. Once in the Reichstag (parliament), he cleverly manoeuvred and orchestrated events so that he could gain more power. He had his men set fire to the parliament buildings and then blamed the fire on the party he considered his main enemy, the Communists. He made people so afraid of the Communists that he easily took power, manoeuvring to have himself named Chancellor, with the promise to "save" the people from the Communists.

Often leaders will use fear of others to gain power for themselves — blaming others and depicting their opponents as evil and dangerous. Hitler did this not only with Communists, but also with Jews. Jews became the scapegoats for all that was wrong in Germany. A bad economy? It must be the Jews' fault. Germany seen as weak by other countries? The Jews' fault. Jews, of course, had no more effect on the economy than any other Germans. But because of long-standing anti-Semitism (prejudice against or hatred of Jews), Hitler was able to perpetuate this lie.

Hitler took this foundation of anti-Semitism and expanded on it. He passed laws that restricted Jews from teaching and from professions such as medicine and law. He passed further laws declaring that Jews could not own businesses; that they could not shop in most places; that they could not walk in a park, swim in a pool, attend school. The courts failed to strike down these laws. Judges upheld them and lawyers argued that they were legal. When no one stood up for the Jews, Hitler began to round them up and to send them to concentration camps. He told the world that he wanted to be rid of Jews and offered to give them away to other countries. But no one wanted them. Canada took in only five thousand during the whole of the Second World War.

Finally Hitler decided to be done with Jews once and for all. He devised the final solution to what he called "the Jewish problem." The final solution was simple. He would exterminate them all.

Death camps, as they came to be known, were places where those who had been rounded up by the Nazi regime were sent to be murdered. At first the locations were work camps, and then often work and death camps, where people were separated on arrival — some sent to do work, some sent to death in the gas chambers, some worked to death.

Buchenwald concentration camp was established in 1937. It was built in Germany near the city of Weimar. When it first opened, political prisoners were sent there, but in 1938 ten thousand Jews were imprisoned, hundreds dying almost immediately due to the harsh treatment they received. As well as Jews and political prisoners, others were also sent there — Jehovah's Witnesses, Roma and Sinti (groups that some people used to call "Gypsies"), and later, prisoners of war, resistance fighters, foreign forced labour and those deemed criminals by the state.

By 1945 one hundred and twelve thousand prisoners were incarcerated. Many were forced to work for the German war machine and Buchenwald became important for its factories, which churned out munitions and other material for the war effort, using forced labour.

168 Allied Airmen

Each of the 168 Allied airmen who ended up in Buchenwald had a different story, in that each was shot down on a different day, at a different time, and had different experiences while hiding in France, trying to evade the enemy. But each was somehow betrayed, or captured by the Germans, and sent to Fresnes Prison in Paris. Even in prison each had a different experience: some were isolated, some were tortured, some were with friends. Some were there for days, others for weeks, even months. From the moment they were put on the train to Buchenwald, their stories intertwined. According to the Geneva Convention, captured Allied airmen should never have been sent to a concentration camp but directly to a prisoner-of-war camp. However, they suffered the same fate as the Resistance fighters.

On October 20, the airmen were removed from Buchenwald and on October 22 they were interned in POW camp Stalag Luft III. On January 28, 1945, Stalag Luft III was evacuated and ten thousand Allied airmen were forced to march away from their liberators, the Russian and American troops that were drawing near. The POWs, or as they called themselves, *Kriegies* (short for *Kriegsgefangener*, or war prisoner in German) had no ability to hold off the evacuation, since they were at the mercy of their German guards. Still, the *Kriegies* walked as slowly as they could and delayed as much as possible, following orders from their group captain, in the hope of being overtaken by the Allies.

At one point RAF fighters mistook the column for retreating German soldiers and strafed them. Some had the presence of mind to dive into a ditch when they saw the planes coming, but others stayed on the road to wave at their liberators. Because of that, some of the *Kriegies* were killed by their own side.

On April 23 some of the airmen found themselves at a large country estate where they were allowed to wait until Allied troops could reach them. They were liberated on May 2 by General Montgomery's 11th Armoured Division. Their war was over!

On May 6 they boarded a transport to England and landed in an airfield north of London. Some of the men were then assigned transport to Bournemouth, and a billet in a hotel where they could clean up and get into new clothes. Then they went out to celebrate Victory in Europe (VE) Day on May 8.

This book is inspired by the true story of the flyers who were shot down, evaded the Germans, were captured and imprisoned in Paris, sent to Buchenwald, and then at the last moment — just before they were to be executed — sent to a POW camp. The flyers were from all the Allied countries.

Canada's National Film Board created a documentary about these men: *The Lucky Ones: Allied Airmen of Buchenwald.* A more recent documentary film by Mike Dorsey titled *Lost Airmen of Buchenwald* uses archival and often secret footage of the plight of these airmen. It held its premiere in 2011, sixty-five years after the captured Allied airmen marched out of Stalag Luft III.

RCAF training prepared students for deadly combat. This photo, taken upon graduation from a school in Mossbank, Saskatchewan, indicates with an "X" those young men who were killed overseas during the war.

Smoke billows below this Lancaster on a bombing run over its target.

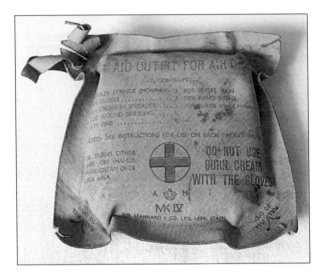

An RAF first-aid kit such as this was given to each flyer. It contained items like burn cream, wound dressings and morphine capsules for pain.

Members of the French Jewish Resistance group Armée Juive stand in their military uniforms.

The small and light Type A MK III suitcase radio was used by operatives of the British Strategic Operations Executive (SOE) to help resistance efforts in Nazi-occupied countries. Its transmission range was approximately 800 km.

SS and police officials during a roll call of Polish concentration camp prisoners.

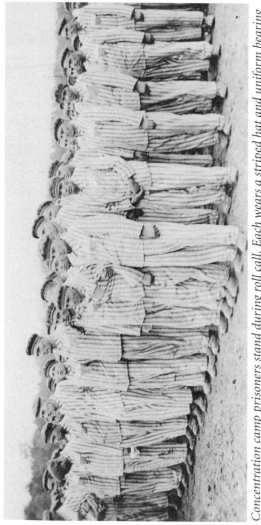

Concentration camp prisoners stand during roll call. Each wears a striped hat and uniform bearing coloured, triangular badges and identification numbers.

Former prisoners of the "little camp" in Buchenwald stare out from the wooden bunks in which they slept three to a bed. Elie Wiesel, Nobel Peace Prize winner and writer of dozens of books about the Holocaust, is in the second row of bunks from the bottom, seventh from the left, next to the vertical beam.

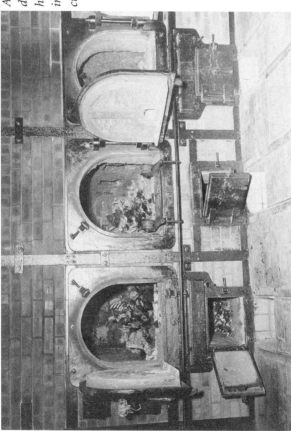

American troops discovered human remains in Buchenwald's crematoria.

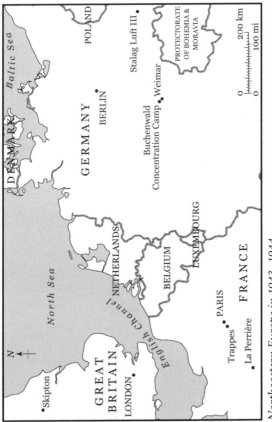

Northeastern Europe in 1943–1944.

Credits

Acknowledgments

My heartfelt thanks to the veterans who helped me with this manuscript, first and foremost John Harvie, Lancaster navigator, one of the 168 airmen shot down over France and later incarcerated in Buchenwald. His book *Missing in Action* was an inspiration, as was his tireless help through many phone calls and emails. I'm sorry to say that he has since passed away. The book *A Fighter Pilot in Buchenwald* by Joe Moser, as told by Gerald R. Baron, is also a wonderful memoir. I listened to a podcast by Harold Bastable, who grew up in Winnipeg and gave talks to students about his wartime experiences. I was also able to read his personal memoir thanks to the generosity of his family. Ed Carter-Edwards answered a question no one else could. Finally, the book *168 Jump into Hell* by Arthur Kinnis and Stanley Booker was written because after the war many did not believe that Allied airmen were actually imprisoned in Buchenwald. So the airmen banded together once again and set out to put the record straight.

I would be remiss to leave out the experts who read the manuscript and helped me correct mistakes and pointed me in the right direction

— many thanks to Carl Christie and all his Air Force contacts, and Professor Robert Young, Trish McNorgan and fact-checker extraordinaire Barb Hehner. I also thank the following airmen who so kindly emailed me with answers to some of my questions: Andrew Christie, Stu Beaton, Robert Vincent, Ernest Cable, Jim Buckland, Jim Bell, William Carr, Fred Aldworth, Jim Shilliday, Cal Shermerhorn, Ernie Drouin, E.V. "Dusty" Titheridge, James Popplow. If there are any mistakes they are mine and mine alone.

And a big thank you to my editor, Sandy Bogart Johnston, for her calm and cool and her tireless attention; my husband Per Brask; and my friend Perry Nodelman for reading the manuscript and for all his suggestions. I also thank the Manitoba Arts Council for the grant, which helped tremendously, giving me the time to research this large project.

Lastly, a word to my readers. This is a book of fiction, although it is based on the story of 168 airmen who were shot down in France in World War II. My character Sam is a fictional character inserted into this group, as are his friends, Max, James, Trent, etc. On the night that Sam is shot down, a Lancaster bomber was actually lost in an op over Trappes, France, but Sam Frederiksen's crew is not based on that one.

About the Author

Carol Matas's parents were born in Canada, but her grandparents and great-grandparents immigrated here from various eastern European countries, thus escaping some of the horrifying events of World War II. Carol's father-in-law, Olaf Brask, was a fighter in the Danish Resistance during that war. Her book *Jesper* is inspired by his story.

Carol is perhaps best known for her Holocaust novels, such as *Daniel's Story* (shortlisted for the Governor General's Award and winner of the Silver Birch Award), *After the War* and *The Garden* (both winners of the Jewish Book Award), *Lisa* (a Geoffrey Bilson Award winner), *Jesper, Greater Than Angels* and *In My Enemy's House*. She has written two Dear Canada books, *Footsteps in the Snow*, about Winnipeg's Red River Settlement, and *Turned Away*, which received the Margaret McWilliams Award from the Manitoba Historical Society. That story highlights Canada's refusal to allow any Jews from Europe into the country during World

War II, as well as the actions of Canadian soldiers who fought at Hong Kong and were either killed or made prisoners of war by the Japanese.

Carol interviewed several of the 168 Allied airmen whose story was the springboard for this novel. When one of the few remaining Lancaster bombers that are still flying landed in Winnipeg in spring 2011, she climbed right inside it, to see what it might have been like for Sam Frederiksen in his position as a gunner.

Carol lives with her family in Winnipeg, Manitoba.

Other books in the
I AM CANADA series

Prisoner of Dieppe
World War II
Hugh Brewster

Blood and Iron
Building the Railway
Paul Yee

Shot at Dawn
World War I
John Wilson

Deadly Voyage
RMS *Titanic*
Hugh Brewster

For more information please see the I AM CANADA
website: www.scholastic.ca/iamcanada